"Transformation doesn't happe[...] work of His Spirit in those who [...] disciples. These disciples are in [...] hidden. With simplicity and integrity, Christy Wimber offers beautiful insights on trust and surrender as the key aspects of how the Father brings transformation to our lives. Christy has written with a vulnerability that will put you in touch with your own deepest desire to be profoundly changed by Jesus. This leads to an identity rooted in the love of a good Father. I highly recommend Transformed as a book that will bring hope and healing for those who find themselves with a desperate yearning for deep and lasting change."

Bill Johnson, Bethel Church, Redding, CA, author of *When Heaven Invades Earth* and *Essential Guide to Healing*

"We at HTB owe so much to John Wimber, whose teaching had a hugely significant impact on our church. Christy Wimber draws much from her father-in-law's teaching as she leads the Vineyard Church at Yorba Linda. I am delighted to hear of her book Transformed and am sure that many people will be drawn to closer relationship with Jesus through reading it."

Nicky Gumbel, founder of Alpha

"Few leaders in today's western church have the length and breadth of experience in the charismatic movement that Christy Wimber has. In her new book Transformed, Christy brings a prophet's challenge, a pastor's care and a teacher's instruction to keep the church in step with the Spirit."

Simon Ponsonby, St Aldates Oxford

"Christy tells the truth. And much like Jesus, she tells it kindly. This book can awaken us to the possibilities of transformation – the struggle and fun, the sweat and grace! And it is written by a women who embodies its content. Read this book if you want to go deeper in your journey with Jesus."

Danielle Strickland, Salvation Army

"The more things change the more they stay the same. In an ever changing world we need to be reminded of the simple clear truths that have held the church steady for centuries. Christy challenges us to steady ourselves in his hope and grace, a much needed encouragement."

Jay Pathak, Founding pastor of the Mile High Vineyard

"I loved this book! It's accessible and hard hitting, but full of grace. It's thought provoking, yet practical. Most of all, it's so refreshingly honest about what following Jesus actually looks like. Transformed is packed with wisdom and insights on how to pursue a deeper spirituality where every part of our life is invested in the pursuit of Jesus and the cause of his kingdom."

Pete Hughes, KXC, London

"The last couple of decades have seen a remarkable cultural shift on an unprecedented global scale. The 'C'hurch, and hence the face of liturgy and the expression of worship, has not gone unchallenged; unchanged; nor unscathed by these seismic shifts. My dear friend; colleague; 'boss' at times; and co-laborer in the Vineyard Movement of churches Christy Wimber, has a unique vantage point in these times, not only able to give an accurate assessment of where we've been, but some pretty great insight into that which we need to celebrate and glean from this season, and that which we need to be wary of and even leave behind as we navigate the future of our understanding and expression of worship. Give it a read. Good stuff."

David Ruis, worship leader and National Director of Vineyard churches, Canada

Check Out Receipt

Poulsbo
360-779-2915
http://www.krl.org

Wednesday, January 9, 2019 1:04:55 PM

Item: 39068028114637
Title: Getting the job you want after 50 f
or dummies
Call no.: 331.702 HANNON
Material: Book
Due: 01/30/2019

Item: 39068029117944
Title: Transformed
Call no.: 248.4 WIMBER 2017
Material: Book
Due: 01/30/2019

Total items: 2

What conversations can we spark?
Read this years One Book selection
Behold the Dreamers by Imbolo Mbue,
then meet the author & join in the
conversation. Details at onebook.KRL.org.

Transformed

CHRISTY WIMBER

MONARCH
BOOKS

Oxford, UK, and Grand Rapids, USA

Published by Monarch Books
an imprint of
Lion Hudson plc
Wilkinson House, Jordan Hill Road,
Oxford OX2 8DR, England
Email: monarch@lionhudson.com
www.lionhudson.com/monarch

ISBN 978 0 85721 812 4
e-ISBN 978 0 85721 813 1

First edition 2017

Acknowledgments

Scripture quotations taken from the Amplified® Bible, Copyright © 1954, 1958, 1962, 1965, 1987 by The Lockman Foundation. Used by permission. Scripture quotations marked ESV are from The Holy Bible, English Standard Version® (ESV®) copyright © 2001 by Crossway, a publishing ministry of Good News Publishers. All rights reserved. Extracts from The Authorized (King James) Version. Rights in the Authorized Version are vested in the Crown. Reproduced by permission of the Crown's patentee, Cambridge University Press. Scripture taken from the New American Standard Bible®, Copyright © 1960, 1962, 1963, 1968, 1971, 1972, 1973, 1975, 1977, 1995 by The Lockman Foundation. Used by permission. Scripture taken from the New Century Version. Copyright © by Thomas Nelson, Inc. Used by permission. All rights reserved. Scripture quotations are taken from the *Holy Bible, New Living Translation*, copyright © 1996, 2004, 2007 by Tyndale House Foundation. Used by permission of Tyndale House Publishers, Inc., Carol Stream, Illinois 60188. All rights reserved. Scripture quotations marked VOICE taken from The Voice™. Copyright © 2008 by Ecclesia Bible Society. Used by permission. All rights reserved. Scripture quotations marked ICB are taken from The Holy Bible, International Children's Bible® Copyright© 1986, 1988, 1999, 2015 by Tommy Nelson™, a division of Thomas Nelson. Thomas Nelson is a registered trademark of HarperCollins Christian Publishing, Inc. Scripture quotations marked Passion Translation are taken from The Passion Translation copyright © 2016. Used by permission of BroadStreet Publishing Group, LLC, Racine, Wisconsin, USA. All rights reserved.thePassionTranslation.com

A catalogue record for this book is available from the British Library

Printed and bound in the US, March 2017, LH37

For my kids: Camie Rose Wimber Johnson, and
John Richard Wimber II.
I love you.

Thank you for your patience with me as I have had to
learn what it means to grow up. Thank you for keeping
your sense of humor, especially when it comes to the
ministry. Thank you for making me laugh at myself and
reminding me not to take things to seriously. Thank
you for the countless hours you spent in airplanes,
airports, conferences, churches, or just waiting for
mommy to be done with work so you could go
home. Most people have no idea the price kids pay
for a parent to be in ministry, but I do because I have
watched you live it. You are a constant reminder of
God's mercy to me.

Thank you for loving me, and letting me love you, and
for always telling me the truth. I wouldn't be who I
am today without the two of you, as you have made
me look at myself in ways I wouldn't have otherwise. I
am beyond grateful that out of all the mommys in the
world God allowed me to be yours.

I love you more than life.
Isaiah 59:21

Contents

Prayer of St. Brendan

Help me to journey beyond the familiar
and into the unknown.

Give me the faith to leave old ways
and break fresh ground with You.

Christ of the mysteries, I trust You
to be stronger than each storm within me.

I will trust in the darkness and know
that my times, even now, are in Your hand.

Tune my spirit to the music of heaven,
and somehow, make my obedience count for You.

Amen.

CHAPTER 1

Sacrifice, sweat, and suffering

The idea that successful media status, fame, money, or visibility will fix our lives and ministries is just an illusion. None of those things make us fruitful, they just reveal whether we have any lasting fruit to begin with.

I WAS WATCHING A CLIP of a well-known movie star, and the interviewer was talking about how great things must be for her; how many people must drool over her amazing life, her fame, and her money. As the interview continued, I noticed the face of the actress changing as the ridiculous questions went on. It was clear that the more her lifestyle was idolized, the more agitated she became, her smile fading to an angry smirk. As she listened to the idealistic interviewer, her response was sharp: "You know, it is an illusion to think that just because someone has money, fame, or whatever they wish they had, that it is a picture of their life in which all is good. Just because you get something, or you know someone, doesn't mean s***. It's all an illusion."

I burst out laughing because of her honesty. But sadly, her statement revealed much truth about today's culture. This idolization of the outward appearance of people's lives has become a powerful illusion. This interview reminded me of what I often see in traveling and teaching around the world. The illusion and celebrity mindset is not just a world mentality; it has slowly crept its way into the church. The focus to become a teacher, pastor, worship leader, or itinerate minister – for the visibility and fame – has become too important. Serving in the local church, just to serve God, has in many ways lost its appeal. It seems as if bigger is better, and having more, or at least looking like you have more, proves that you're successful and living the American Dream!

Social media can create the illusion that everything is bigger or better than it actually is. These posts encourage the false beliefs that all is well, that no one truly struggles, and everyone has it better than us. These are messages that we're constantly being fed through the media. Whether we realize it or not, this kind of influence has impacted the church and what we think of ourselves, our ministries, and even our own personal lives. Time and time again, I hear from people who feel that they are "less than" others in what they do, or who they are as a person. There are many discouraged leaders who feel that what they do isn't big enough, or significant enough, compared to what they've seen happening around the world – mostly from the Internet of course.

However, as with most things concerning the Internet, the reality is often different to what is being portrayed. I can't tell you how many times I read something about a church only to show up and find that what they say about themselves is very different to how it actually is. It's like a bad online dating service, where people present themselves in a certain way so they get attention, yet in person, the reality is not quite the same as the advertisement! It not only surprises, but also saddens me, how often I hear the pressure people feel to keep up with others. We want to look good, telling ourselves, "At least I'm growing with Twitter or Facebook followers", and worrying about how many "likes" we got on a post – as if any of that really matters.

WHEN THERE IS SO MUCH FOCUS ON THE OUTWARD, IT IS EASY TO FALL INTO A TRAP, GIVING THE FALSE ILLUSION THAT WE ARE A DEEPER AND STRONGER CHRISTIAN THAN WE REALLY ARE.

We feed the cry for surface life by giving surface responses. Yet I find it interesting that when I ask younger generations what they love about people, especially leaders, who have followed Jesus for years, I often find the same answers. In fact, I find they are the same qualities that I love and am attracted to myself.

Longevity, morality, and integrity are the things which attract us the most. There is a deep desire within all of us to finish well. We are dying for positive role models to represent the godly mothers and fathers who are often missing in the home. We are made to be in a family, where we can have people to look up to; not just to admire, but to model our lives on. I also believe that is why the young are so drawn to people with those deep qualities; they represent safety, and we all want to feel safe. There is a deep need, all around us, with so many searching and longing for mothers and fathers, and if the church isn't filling the need, the world is quick to offer a counterfeit replacement.

Even in our own resistance and self-reliance, we are wired

for the long-term and to be called into a deep and authentic relationship with Christ. No one imagines their life will turn out poorly; for the most part everyone wants to produce a healthy life, healthy children, and a healthy deposit into society. Yet everything in and around us is fighting this. Culture is stealing our attention towards immediate gratifications, rather than the bigger picture of what has eternal value.

Eugene Peterson, in his book *A Long Obedience in the Same Direction*, said this: "There is a great market for religious experience in our world; there is little enthusiasm for the patient acquisition of virtue, little inclination to sign up for a long apprenticeship in what earlier generations of Christians called holiness."[1]

In our instant, microwave culture we like things to be fast. We like things to be done for us, and to have everything at our beck and call when we want it. If people or places don't produce what we want here and now, then we'll find somewhere else that will. Don't get me wrong, I love the microwave and I love it when things are quick and easy, but spiritual depth, or spiritual maturity, is not something we can just order online; if it was, we would!

There is nothing about discipleship where "fast", "easy", "convenient", or even "comfortable" would be words used to describe the journey. In fact, where we find the strongest, deepest, and healthiest growth, there has been a journey of sacrificial choices of transformation behind the scenes.

THE BEST THINGS, THINGS WHICH HAVE THE GREATEST VALUE, ARE NEVER WITHOUT SACRIFICE.

---

1   Eugene H. Peterson, *A Long Obedience in the Same Direction: Discipleship in an Instant Society*, Downers Grove, IL: IVP Books, 2000, p. 16.

Jesus modelled this for us in His earthly ministry all the way to the cross. He made it clear that we are His greatest value. We were the object of His sacrifice. We have such great worth to Him, and where we find the greatest of worth is where we find the greatest of investments. God will invest in that which matters most. That's why every great leader we read about through the Scriptures had to allow God to put His best investments in them. God never just threw them into big missions; before He released responsibility, there was always training in the hidden place, either with God directly, or with others who could walk them through the process.

Joseph had to wait thirteen years for his prophetic promise to be revealed. God gave him a dream, yet his immaturity got him thrown into a pit; he had to walk through many trials, betrayals, and rejections before he was entrusted with the palace. David went from being a shepherd boy in the field, to being anointed by Samuel, only to be sent back into the field again. Even when he was called up for service, I'm sure it was different to how he had planned, as he had to serve crazy King Saul, and if that wasn't enough he had to go on the run for his life for years. He went through many seasons of painful circumstances until he found himself in the role of king. Likewise, in the New Testament, we find that the apostle Paul had to wait for several years after his conversion before he was commissioned into ministry. We find story after story of God's giants being trained in the hidden places. The hidden place is not what we would pick, but it is often the place God can do His best work in us. It's the deepest and sometimes longest of investments and sometimes we need to remember that the best things in life are often found where we have put our greatest investments.

Psalm 1 is one of my favorites. It promises that we have the potential to be like "a tree firmly planted by streams of water, which yields its fruit in its season and its leaf does not wither; and in whatever he does, he prospers" (Psalm 1:3 NASB).

To prosper is God's idea. Too often we have taken what the world sees as prosperity, and put the stamp of Jesus on it. God wants you to prosper but His ways do not follow the patterns of this world. He is of another kingdom.

THE WORD "PROSPER" HERE MEANS MORE THAN TO PROFIT AND BE SUCCESSFUL; IT ALSO MEANS TO SHOW EXPERIENCE.

I love this Scripture because it gives the picture that wherever God plants us, it doesn't matter what life throws our way; we will prosper in it.

However, to prosper doesn't mean that life is easy. We have confused God's blessing with things being easy. We have confused the best fruit of our lives as that which is quickest and tastiest, yet some of the best fruit takes the longest time to grow.

John 15 gives us the picture of staying connected to our life source, the vine. Jesus tells us: "I am the vine, you are the branches; he who abides in Me and I in him, he bears much fruit, for apart from Me you can do nothing" (John 15:5 NASB). As with any fruit that grows, it cannot sustain itself apart from the vine. God's kingdom flourishes in those who choose to stay attached to the Vine. There is not a promise of a particular length of time, only the choice to stay attached, where we can allow our roots to go deep in Christ. Our deepest strength is found in the strength of our roots; the deeper the root, the deeper the strength of what is being produced.

SOME OF THE BEST THINGS GOD HAS FOR US TAKE THE LONGEST TO GROW. THE OLD SAYING, THE FRUIT OF OUR LABOR, MEANS JUST THAT: FRUIT IS A BY-PRODUCT OF LABOR.

I am sure that Joseph, David, and Paul were wondering why the process had to take so long, yet they still walked it out. They continued to give God their "yes" even though they had to persevere for years and through life-threatening problems. It was because of their "yes" that God used them greatly. God spoke to all of these men, and many others, yet they still had to surrender to the process. They had to yield and allow God to transform them into who they were called to be.

GETTING POWER IS EASY; DIRECTING IT IN THE WAY IT'S INTENDED MUST BE LEARNED THROUGH A PROCESS.

Hearing from God about your life is one thing, but getting yourself ready for what God has said is a completely different ball game. Receiving a prophetic word that you're going to do, or be, something that you've dreamed of may encourage you, but that is only the beginning of your story. After the word, we often have to persevere through many problems before we get to the promise. Most people get the word and think "that's it, here I am", and expect every door to open – when in fact that word is just the reminder of the promise. That's actually what the prophetic means: *to build up, to exhort, to encourage,* even *to bring comfort.*

PROPHETIC WORDS ARE NOT FOR CORRECTION OR DIRECTION, THEY ARE TO ENCOURAGE YOU TO KEEP FOCUSED, AND KEEP PERSEVERING – KEEPING YOUR EYE ON THE PROMISE OF GOD. IF YOU DON'T KEEP PERSEVERING, THEN DON'T EXPECT THE PROMISE.

Have you ever been under a leader who had power but misused it? It doesn't matter if it is through parenting, leading a church, driving a bus, or being a doctor; misdirected power can do so much damage. The training is not only for ourselves, the training is for everyone around us as well.

THE POWER THAT GOD PLACES IN YOUR LIFE HAS RESPONSIBILITY ATTACHED TO IT, AND IF YOU DON'T ALLOW GOD'S SPIRIT TO BREAK YOU IN THIS PROCESS, THEN THAT POWER CAN DO MUCH DAMAGE.

Romans chapter 5 says this is the road to true character and hope: "suffering produces perseverance; perseverance, character; and character, hope" (Romans 5:3–4). Power and position, without character or hope as their path, are destructive. Perseverance is always a process, and it's usually a hidden one, because God is doing a deep work in the roots of who we are; roots, and seeds, the things that give life, strength, and stability, are hidden. But if they aren't cared for and grown properly, they cannot contain what they're meant to carry. The hidden process is not popular in today's culture. No one can "like" your process. It goes against popular culture, even in the church. We often try to make things sound more exciting, or faster, than the reality; however, **God's timing and our timing are usually worlds apart.**

Can you imagine if King David was alive today? How many Facebook or Twitter fans do you think he would have, being a shepherd boy in a field? He would probably be perceived as rather boring, singing and talking to God and his sheep! The processes, especially long ones, are not popular, yet it is the way God trains those He calls His own.

Every person God entrusted with a significant task had to go through this hidden process of training. It is part of His entrustment program. If I was doing twenty-five years ago what I am doing today, I would have done a lot of damage. I would have hurt people. Not on purpose, but I just didn't have the maturity for what I lead today. I had to go through a much-needed process of training to learn that it's not only what I see that is important, but what I do with what I see. In other words, God may reveal things to me about people that are true, yet if I don't share those things in grace, they can be hurtful. I needed to work on the grace part.

THESE SEASONS OF BEING HIDDEN, OFTEN SERVING UNDER TRYING CIRCUMSTANCES, ARE WHERE GOD DOES HIS BEST WORK IN US. THESE ARE USUALLY TIMES THAT WE WOULD NEVER PICK, USING PEOPLE WE WOULD NEVER CHOOSE, IN ORDER FOR GOD TO WORK IN US IN WAYS THAT COULDN'T HAPPEN OTHERWISE.

Psalm 27:14 says, "Don't give up, don't be impatient, be entwined as one with the Lord. Be brave, courageous, and never lose hope. Yes, keep on waiting – for He will never disappoint you." In this Passion Translation, the waiting time is not wasted time; rather it is a secluded time for God to form our inner man. The Hebrew word for wait means to entwine like strands of rope being woven into one. That is not an easy process.

God tells us that He is the potter and we are the clay. The great Creator is fully aware of what we are made to be. Isaiah 29:16 (NLT) says, "How foolish can you be? He is the Potter, and he is certainly greater than you, the clay! Should the created thing say of the one who made it, 'He didn't make me'? Does a jar ever say, 'The potter who made me is stupid'?"

Have you ever seen pottery being made? It is often beaten, and even thrown to the ground, in order for it to take shape. It's not that God is beating us up, but He is allowing us to be formed, and to be worked into His image. None of that is an easy process, yet it is vital to become what we have been made to be.

It is normal to feel as if you are the only one having to walk through your situation. These hidden times of God working in us are often lonely times because God is at work in our private places, so rarely is anyone watching, let alone applauding.

True change is not a status change on social media. True change takes sacrifice, sweat, and even suffering – three things I hardly ever hear mentioned in church, or at conferences, these days. They are not the popular topics. In fact, on more than a few occasions, when I've been talking about suffering, I have seen the disapproval of those who are wishing I would do more exciting things, like tell testimonies of healing, rather than address some of the realities of discipleship. It is not popular to talk about struggle. It is not popular to address the suffering we often have to walk through, or the sacrifices we must continually make in order to say "yes" to Jesus.

These things are not popular in today's church culture. We would much rather focus on the successes of life, going from one testimony to the next, even using the saying "it gives the devil too much credit" as an excuse not to address hardship of any kind.

> THE REALITY IS THAT LIFE IS NOT PLAYED OUT LIKE A HIGHLIGHT REEL FROM A CHRISTIAN CONFERENCE.

I love testimonies, and I love celebrating what God's up to. But God is working in the one who has chosen to persevere through pain and loss, just as through the miracle of eyes being healed. So let's celebrate, but not at the expense of those who are faithfully struggling on, whose testimony wasn't as exciting as someone who was healed. Both are equally important.

It's alright to admit that life is sometimes hard. I think it is OK to say we don't necessarily like the season that we're in, or even that we're disappointed that God did not heal the person we love. If we don't allow space for this type of honesty then the church is crippling herself.

Many of the things we go through, and others around us go through, are often very difficult, very painful, and sometimes humiliating. Where do they go for help? Where do we go if we don't feel safe enough to tell the truth about our situations? As a leader, and as a pastor, I want people to choose the narrow road of discipleship. I want them to risk; I want them to thrive in their calling. But if my heart is for people to be honest, and if I want to reproduce a deeper church, then I have to keep asking myself these questions: Am I a safe person? Is my church a safe place? Are we reproducing disciples? If we aren't, then what needs to change?

I don't want to keep up an appearance which in the long run helps no one. All around the world, I see a drive to keep up appearances, and I believe it is taking its toll on the fruit of the church.

WE CANNOT EXPECT TO TREAT PEOPLE, ESPECIALLY SPIRITUAL LEADERS, AS CELEBRITIES, AND THEN BE SURPRISED BY THE LACK OF DISCIPLES IN THE CHURCH. CHOOSING OUR LEADERS BECAUSE OF CHARISMA AND MEDIA INFLUENCE MAY PRODUCE A WIDER CHURCH, BUT NOT A DEEPER ONE.

And it's only a deeper church which can outlast every season. It is the narrow road. It has never been the popular road to follow. Growing true character, and allowing God to do His best work in us, is a choice, not a popularity contest. The narrow road is the road less travelled for a reason. Even though it's not the popular road, it is the road where longevity in true depth of discipleship is found. There is no truth to someone's life being better than ours, or the theory that the grass is greener on the other side.

THE GRASS IS NEVER GREENER WITH SOMEONE OR SOMEPLACE ELSE, THE GRASS IS GREEN WHERE YOU CHOOSE TO WATER IT.

I want to encourage you, as I often have to encourage myself: let the Master do His work in you. Allow Him to mold and transform you into your destiny. Do you realize that no matter where you're at today, God can do something with your "yes"? God can move in you, He can change you, and His promise is to complete His work in you. But you have to give Him your "yes".

Every choice you make is either transforming you into the likeness of Christ and leading you into your destiny, or stealing your purpose and what God has created you for. It's one choice at a time. Don't waste time focusing on how long it is taking for you to get through the season you're in, or looking for a way out. Instead ask for God's strength to empower you to stay. If God is working in you, then no matter what it is, it's for a reason. Every training session has purpose which will save us down the road. This is not a path you want to cut short.

There is a story about a man who was watching a moth trying to break out of its cocoon, and he felt sorry about the effort the little guy had to make, so he grabbed some scissors and cut it out. But as the moth began to move he realized it didn't have the strength to fly. In this man's attempt to help the little moth, he actually crippled it. The moth needs the struggle because the struggle builds in it what it needs in order to fly. This is what it looks like when we try to take shortcuts. In the long run it hurts us, and sometimes others as well.

There is no such thing as quick maturity. If you want your life to show experience, you must face, head on, where God has you today. If you want to prosper, you must plant yourself, attach yourself to the Vine, and allow your roots to go deep. I want to encourage you to fight for the things that last long-term, the things that matter the most. Ask yourself, what will be important 100 years from now? What are the things that truly last in life and ministry? What are the things that have lasted and benefited family life from generation to generation?

Then ask yourself, is my life connected to, and invested in, such things?

CHAPTER 2

What Jesus did I say "yes" to?

You have to know the Jesus you said "yes" to, because the Jesus you said "yes" to is the Jesus you'll end up following.

I LOVE SEASONS. It wasn't always like that, as growing up in southern California we have two seasons: hot and hotter! However, as I've traveled around the world I have grown to love the seasons, even winter, although that's probably because I don't live somewhere where I end up having to dig my car out of deep snow every day! When I was a child one of my favorite things to do when it was really hot was to sit inside the sweltering car without turning the air conditioning on. Crazy, I know. It's a wonder I survived. If I did that now, I think it would kill me!

Seasons are a way of life and part of the natural world that God created. They are also part of our spiritual life. In the book of Ecclesiastes, we learn that "there is a time for everything, and a season for every activity under the heavens" (Ecclesiastes 3:1).

The chapter continues to explain those seasons; some of them wonderful, and some very difficult, but each one is important. Each time has its purpose and meaning. Our God never wastes anything; even the things that we would rather forget or discount, He has an amazing way of using for a purpose.

Often, especially when we find ourselves in a season we would rather avoid, God is working out His plan for good. It's just who He is.

WE HAVE ALL BEEN IN SEASONS THAT WE CAN'T WAIT TO GET THROUGH, BUT NO MATTER HOW DIFFICULT, THERE IS PURPOSE IN IT. MANY TIMES WHILE WE ARE PLANNING OUR ESCAPE, GOD IS PLANNING HIS PURPOSE.

Seasons are not something we need to just "get through"; each season matters because they are part of the world God has created. They affect every part of life; in fact, you may start this book in one season of your life, and end it in another.

There have been many seasons in my life where it was beautiful, and thoroughly enjoyable: when my children were born, when I saw people meet with Jesus for the first time, or when I watched God doing what He does best, bringing healing and restoration to people who are at the end of their rope. I've walked through seasons of grace, where God has come through on personal things, and without His intervention, I would not have made it. I have countless wonderful memories of relaxing with my family; watching my children grow up, graduate from school, and especially watching my daughter get married, are seasons and moments that are deeply imbedded in my memory. I can even look back at times of deep sorrow, when I've watched those I love pass from their physical life to their eternal life with Jesus, and see those too as seasons of God's grace. Watching someone you love become at peace, seeing their countenance at rest, is a gift, a moment of grace. All of these moments, and all of these seasons, have formed who I am. You all have your own seasons and your own memories, but no matter the joy or difficulty of those times, each of them formed who you are.

The hardest thing about a life of seasons is that we don't get to pick which season we are in, or how long it lasts for. We only get to pick how we choose to respond to the season we're in, knowing all the while that God always has our "yes". My last season has been a winter season for me, where I have felt extremely frail and exposed. Although I knew God was at work, and fruit was being produced, it was really hard for me to see it. I don't think I did anything particularly wrong, but every time I thought it was coming to an end, something else would happen – often something very painful to me personally, or to someone I love.

YOU DON'T HAVE TO BE DOING ANYTHING WRONG TO ENCOUNTER HARDSHIP. WE WANT TO BLAME SOMEONE OR SOMETHING, EVEN OURSELVES, BUT SOMETIMES OUR GREATEST HARDSHIPS COME WHEN WE ARE DOING EXACTLY WHAT GOD HAS ASKED US TO DO.

For me this last season was full of non-stop opposition. Each time I turned around, I could barely catch my breath before another hit came. I wish these seasons didn't exist, but they do, and they happen to all of us.

These are the times when I appreciate that God has wired me in a way that I seem able to handle a lot of opposition without it distracting me too much. This has been a God-given strength for me, but as with any strength, it has been a weakness as well. Sometimes I have the ability to handle *too* much. The season was starting to wear me down, and even though it takes a lot for me to get discouraged, facing *so many* discouragements all at once was taking a toll on my soul. I felt as if I was coming to a breaking point.

We all have something that breaks through our resistance, and for me it has to do with my kids. My "mom" hat overrides everything, and can bring me to my knees rather quickly. If either of my kids is hurting or struggling I feel it deeply. In particular, my son John has dealt with health issues his entire life. I don't understand why. I don't understand why it hasn't stopped, and more specifically, I don't understand why God hasn't healed him, especially when I personally have prayed for people with some of the same conditions he has suffered with and I've seen *them* healed. This is one of those things I'll have to ask Jesus about one day. For now, however, this is what we deal with, sometimes non-stop, and when we do, it brings me to my knees, wishing I could take his place.

One of these difficult moments came when we were already facing tough opposition in other areas, and now here my boy was, suffering again. I was sitting in a hospital room, watching him, and I could tell that my heart was starting to feel the effects of the season. I was angry. The previous day, on my way back to the hospital, I had been involved in a four-car pile-up. I was bruised and discouraged, and began to question many things about my life and ministry. I had been facing serious harassment by the landlord of our church, with hundreds of false accusations and ongoing battles over a two-year period. Every time I returned home from a trip there would be yet another list of accusations, and the effort and the cost to continue defending myself and my church were beyond exhausting. Relationally I was hurt deeply. I had personally invested in and trusted people who were now going sideways, or choosing not to follow through on agreements. Although I was feeling the weight of these things personally, I was more concerned about how these people's poor choices were going to affect those I was leading. To call this season a nightmare would be a massive understatement.

In the midst of the chaos I was trying to hear God, and I felt overwhelmed at the thought of missing Him completely – what if I was going through all of this for nothing? Have you ever tried to hear God, yet the noise around you seems to be drowning Him out? It's a very frustrating season to walk through. As I was lying down next to my boy in the hospital room I just began to tell the Lord about all my frustrations, discouragements, and disillusionments. My list was longer than I realized, and I was quickly sliding into self-pity. Yet I sensed the Lord was just listening to my battered soul. After releasing my long list of complaints, I felt the Lord simply remind me of what He had spoken to me at an earlier time.

I had been doing a conference in late 2015 and during one of the breaks I had gone on a walk to rest and talk to the Lord about a few things. There was something that I didn't quite understand at the time, and His response surprised me: "Christy, what Jesus did you sign up to follow?" What Jesus did I sign up to follow? I kept asking myself that, because it felt like a challenge as well as a reminder, and it still does, every time I think of it.

WE HAVE TO KNOW THE JESUS THAT WE SIGNED UP TO FOLLOW, BECAUSE THE JESUS WE SAID "YES" TO IS THE JESUS WE WILL END UP FOLLOWING.

If we said "yes" to Jesus believing everything was going to be easy, or that it would all turn out how we wanted, then disappointment was sure to follow.

I've heard people say "yes" to Jesus because of a moment of excitement at a conference or because He makes them feel good, or because of the experience of being prayed for. None of these things are bad, but if you say "yes" to Jesus because of an experience, or a feeling, what happens when the feelings aren't there? What happens when the feelings change? I think on some occasions, the church has done a disservice to people by offering them a different Jesus to the Jesus of the Bible. You have to know the Jesus you said "yes" to.

Watching how people respond to life's circumstances reveals very quickly which Jesus they said "yes" to. On one hand it's been a good reminder, because it has always caused me to be sober about the reality of how easy it is for *any* of us to follow the Jesus of convenience and comfort. One thing I noticed was that there were people who were surprised by having to walk through difficulty – strong believers, who had walked and prayed with others in similar hardships, but the moment *they* were faced with such difficulties, it seemed to sweep them off their feet: *"Why me? Why am I having to walk through this? I've done what I thought was right, I've tried to obey God, so why is this happening to me?"*

Could it be that deep down, we feel that the Jesus we said "yes" to, and the Jesus we are willing to follow, to serve, and to risk for, is OK – as long as He works inside our idea of what life should look like? I call it the "as long as… I will say 'yes' to Jesus" theory. As long as I have money; as long as the kids are healthy; as long as I don't have to change too much; as long as my friends come along;

as long as… We all have our lists. These "as long as" reasons have derailed many wonderful people.

Jesus doesn't work within our "as long as" ideas of Christianity. He even forewarned us, "If you say 'yes' to me, it will cost you. It may cost you some friends, it may even cost you some of your family relationships, but don't be surprised if people hate you because of me" (based on Luke 21:16–17).

THE COST IS HIGH BECAUSE THE BENEFITS ARE HIGH. EVERYTHING THAT JESUS WARNED US ABOUT INVOLVES AN ELEMENT OF LIVING UNCOMFORTABLY.

Don't be surprised when things turn out differently to how we expected. Why do we get surprised when we encounter hardships, or when people don't like us? God even warns us of persecution, of rejection, and of the ongoing choice to leave comfort behind. But Christ is all-provisional: in life and in ministry. He has promised us His Spirit, who is our comforter. As believers, we are meant to live in the uncomfortable places. Otherwise, why would we need to be comforted? We know the "Father of compassion and the God of all comfort, who comforts us in all our troubles, so that we can comfort those in any trouble with the comfort we ourselves receive from God" (2 Corinthians 1:3–4). This tells me, in fact, that if I am comfortable, something is wrong.

It's not always the distractions of hardship that cause people to disengage. One of the greatest reasons for distance in our walk with God, and others, is when things are going really well! It is very easy to get so busy with work and with family that we have not allowed any room to rest. Sometimes we feel that because we only have a limited amount of time after we have done all these things, we have to eliminate something, and often what we cut out is community and church.

"BUSY" IS THE NEW EXCUSE, BUT IT CAN BE FATAL TO OUR WALK WITH GOD. I HAVE FOUND THAT IF I AM TOO BUSY FOR THE RIGHT THINGS, THEN I AM JUST TOO BUSY.

Our relationship with God, as with any relationship, must get our time, and our energy, or it will not work. Your relationship with God won't strengthen itself without your daily involvement. One of the most powerful protections you have is the power to say "no". You have to be able to say "no" to the wrong things, to make the needed time, space, and energy to say "yes" to the right things. Being too busy has been one of the biggest distractions in my own life.

We often think it will be the big disappointments of life which will take us off course, yet I have found through the years in pastoring that it is often in the busyness and distractions of life that people begin to distance themselves from God and church. It's the ongoing distractions of daily life where distance from God and His church takes place. Add success in business and you've got another layer to deal with. The enemy will try to steal your time with success just as much as with the temptations of sin. The enemy is alive and well, not only quick to discourage and distance us in hardship, but also waiting at the door of success. The devil is waiting for you after God uses you. Keeping our heart clean wherever God has placed us, in life and in ministry, is important, but being alert after ministry saves us. I have found that I am the most vulnerable after God has used me in great ways. I am more prone to pride, taking credit for things only God can do. There is an intimacy in exposing yourself when you are ministering to others.

MINISTRY IS NOT JUST ABOUT GETTING MY HEART READY TO GO AND MINISTER, BUT ALSO PROTECTING MY HEART FOLLOWING ANY MINISTRY IS JUST AS IMPORTANT.

I can easily retreat into myself, and become distracted by what's been successful. Isolation from God and church is never an overnight process but rather a slow, daily choice to give our time and our belief systems to things that cause distance. The retreat is just the final step of a slow process that has been happening in someone's life over time. Everyone has to fight against feelings of retreat.

Retreating doesn't even mean that we have to leave the church – some have found it easier to retreat within the church, where all looks fine, but the heart is cut off from anything new. I can think of many times where I've had to fight the desire to hide in the corner under the false illusion I am protecting myself. Many of you reading this are fighting that feeling now, and some of you feel like you fight it all the time.

THE ENEMY'S TACTICS ARE TO ISOLATE US, AND RETREAT IS ONE OF HIS CONSISTENT METHODS. ISOLATION KILLS, AND THE ENEMY UNDERSTANDS THAT – WHICH IS WHY HE USES IT.

I think it's a good thing to remember those who have gone before us, even those where their choices haven't been good as it reminds us to be aware as well as careful. At the very least it reminds us that no one is above anything at any time. I have had to work through the disappointment of watching many who I grew up with, and did life with, slowly retreat into their own lives of busyness or even bitterness. It is difficult to watch people who were once full of passion for God choosing instead to be too busy for God. Even sadder has been watching people get bitter with life, bitter at the church, or bitter at God. To this day I hear from those who are still blaming God, or the church, for their difficulties.

I don't think we talk enough in the church about the reality of the battle that we're in. We need to remember that there is a real enemy, and he has one goal in mind with each of us: to take us out. So whether it is through life's circumstances being difficult, or people disappointing us in various ways, if we are not on guard, we too can easily retreat into safe zones.

We should not be surprised by our lack of understanding, yet often we are. It's literally a waste of time and energy to try to figure it all out. Yet, we still try to figure everything out. If God says: "my thoughts are not your thoughts, neither are your ways my ways" (Isaiah 55:8), it clearly means we will not understand most of what we walk through. Many times I have been caught off guard by what I've had to encounter, but I've been even more surprised to realize that I am not trusting God as much as I thought I was.

EVERY TIME WE STEP FORWARD IN DISCIPLESHIP, IT IS ANOTHER CHOICE TO TRUST GOD IN A WAY WE MAY NOT HAVE HAD TO TRUST HIM BEFORE.

Responding to the Lord

The Jesus we said "yes" to always gets revealed by our responses to life. It's where we find out what we truly believe. Isn't it frustrating when you see something come up in your life that you thought was long gone? We dread the mirror's reflection, being faced with our own weakness, especially weaknesses we thought we'd already dealt with. Every step of trust brings another weak area to the surface. Every season we face, we need another level of God's comfort that we may not have needed before. God has no problem touching areas in your life which have to do with control and insecurity. It is not to shame you, but rather to reveal an area of your heart where you may not have trusted Him before.

With trust, we often don't realize how much – or little – we are actually trusting, until we encounter new areas of life where more is needed. Every time I think I'm fully trusting God, He shows me an area where I have placed my trust in myself or other things.

WHEN GOD REVEALS THINGS TO US THAT NEED TO CHANGE, IT'S NEVER TO DISCOURAGE, BUT RATHER TO ENCOURAGE US INTO PURPOSE.

God never wastes anything, even those times that we wish we could forget. To surrender to Christ means that He can take whatever we've faced on our journey, and use it for tremendous purpose. He always takes the ash of our lives and turns it into a thing of beauty. But beautiful things only come when we give God access to the areas of our life that we have never given Him access to before.

We often ask for more of God's Spirit, thinking it's to see the dead raised, forgetting that the dead person is often us. When God's moving on me, I don't see how great I am, or all that I can do. I see how evil my heart actually is, and experience again the shock and awe that God would not only have mercy on me, but also chooses to use me. It rattles my brain every time I am reminded just how many times God has had mercy on me.

In order for us to see the greatness of our God, we first must recognize just how sinful and lost we really are. There are only two options in our response to Christ: we are either running into Him, or running away from Him. We are either moving forward, or going backwards. There is no such thing as being idle in the kingdom of God. His kingdom is advancing, it is moving forward. Often we take three steps forward and two steps back, and feel like nothing has happened, or nothing is changing. But that's not true! Advancing is advancing, even if it's one step at a time. No person walks through life without having setbacks. In fact, **setbacks are truly a good sign, as it means the enemy is trying to shut down that area where you are changing. He is fully aware that if you trust God in that area of your life, it will do damage to his kingdom. The enemy doesn't waste his time on things that don't affect him or disrupt his world.**

Kingdom life is about occupation. We know who won the battle for our lives, and we know who wins in the end. So the battle isn't about the destination, the battle is about who gets to occupy you and the places where God has put you. When the Spirit of God is moving, He begins to reveal areas in us that must die, sometimes things that we would rather not have exposed. The exposure to what needs to change, the unknown territories we visit, the prodding and probing of God drawing us, and desiring us to go deeper into Him can make us feel like God is asking too much of us. I have felt this numerous times in my own walk with God, and also in praying for many who are surprised by what God is asking of them. The choice to yield to the unknown, or the uncomfortable, is not often what people are thinking about when they say "yes" to Jesus.

In this kingdom journey we are learning to yield every part of who we are, so God can use us to occupy others for Himself. The enemy doesn't make it easy. Occupying any new territory in our own heart never happens without a battle or resistance. When God is at work in us, you can bet the enemy is close by trying to distract, discredit, or discourage us from going forward. We often forget that to have more of God means that we will encounter more of the same things that Jesus Himself encountered during His earthly ministry. **Reading through the Gospels, we find what Jesus lived with. We often highlight the miracles, forgetting that every miracle was surrounded by opposition of some kind.** There is no great move of God in us, or around us, without the enemy doing all he can to shut it down.

The important thing to remember is that as long as we are saying "yes" to Jesus, then things are happening. It's a process of growth; it's a journey where only in His grace and His mercy are we truly able to see what He wants us to see. Every circumstance, every trial, every encounter is an invitation to more of God.

God's routes

He is a "lamp unto my feet, and a light unto my path", Psalm 119:105 (KJV) tells us. One of my favorite reminders about God's leading is found in Exodus 13. The Israelites have been in slavery for over 400 years and now they're finally about to set out for the Promised Land. Moses has the new directions, and he goes back to the people to let them know what God has said. They're about to cross the sea. When they were first set free, they didn't realize the path would be different to what they had in their mind, they just said "yes". It's clear because they responded in fear every time new directions came.

You have to picture this: here they are, all gathered, and the cloud starts to move. They begin to march, but then as they look, the cloud is heading in the wrong direction. At least in their minds it's the wrong direction. The Promised Land is one way, but the cloud is headed the other way. I can imagine how Moses is feeling. I can hear the people begin to grumble, something they did so well, especially when things turned out differently to how they expected. Now the big question arises: Will the people be able to follow? If the directions are different to what they had in their minds, will they still keep going? Will they obey God's words?

This chapter is incredibly revealing about how our God knows just how fragile and insecure we are. Here the people set out, but because of God's great love for them, He chooses to take them on a different route. This is the God that loves them so much that He refuses to lead them in the way that would be the easiest. He refuses to take them the way that would make more sense, at least to them. What's even crazier is that there is another route that's shorter. But that's not what God is doing. Instead He is taking them a different way. Will they follow?

When God leads you in a direction that is different to what you had planned, how do you respond?

What looks like more hardship for the people is actually the deep love and mercy of God. In verse 17 it says that God chose to do this because he knew if they saw war, they would run: "If they face war, they might change their minds." Another version says, "lest the people change their purpose when they see war" (AMPC). In other words, they would go back into slavery.

GOD KNOWS US ALL TOO WELL. MANY TIMES WHEN WE FACE HARDSHIP WE TEND TO RUN BACK INTO WHAT'S FAMILIAR OR WHAT'S EASIER.

See, the people knew that at least back in slavery they would get fed. At least in slavery they knew what their days would look like. At least in slavery there weren't a lot of surprises. God knew that they weren't strong enough to face the unforeseen hardships, and if they did, they would turn from Him and lose their purpose. So what seems like God being harsh is actually Him showing great mercy. He knows the people don't have enough faith, and they don't yet have what it takes to face war. Even though they are no longer slaves, they still have to learn what it means to live and think like a free person.

I've found many times that God will take us on a track that although in the natural it doesn't make sense, it could in fact be the road that will save us. We want the shorter route, we want the easier route, yet God knows our weak areas and the places within us that need to be strengthened for the next season. If you are being rerouted, it's the mercy of God on you. It may not feel like it, but if it is God's leading, it's always the best way. We will never understand all of God's ways, and we don't see everything that God sees. It is only the sovereignty of God that is able to see our past and where we have come from; our current situation and what we need now; but also our future.

GOD IS THE ONE WHO KNOWS THAT OUR GREATEST DESTINY WILL BE FOUND NOT ON THE EASIER ROAD, BUT ON THE ROAD WHERE WE ENCOUNTER WHAT WE NEED FOR STRENGTH, TRUST, AND PERSEVERANCE TO DO THEIR WORK IN US.

This is why we have to know who the leader of our lives is. Knowing this in advance leaves no room for options or negotiations, only willful obedience. If God has you on a road less travelled, you want to stay on that road until He takes you elsewhere. To bail out from a direction that God has ordained will only keep you on that road, even if the surroundings look different. I don't think the destination, or our comfort, is as important to the Lord as our trust and dependence upon Him. There is always purpose in where God has you. Don't waste the road you're on trying to find out why, but rather focus on the purpose in being on the road, and keep going until the work has been completed and God gives you new directions. God will never lead you and then leave you. He promises to be with you forever. He is Immanuel, God with us. So on your journey, even if you feel alone, you never are.

I've found that no matter what road we're on, if we go in the direction that God is leading us, He'll take us where we need to go at just the right time. His timing is always perfect. Proverbs 3:5–6 reminds us to, "Trust in the Lord with all your heart, and lean not on your own understanding; in all your ways acknowledge Him, and He shall direct your paths" (NKJV). This is a great promise of God's provision in direction. As long as we're acknowledging where the Holy Spirit is leading, He will always put us on the right path; even if it is not the path we were expecting, we can rest assured of this truth, no matter what season we find ourselves in.

The reality of life is that there will always be seasons of change. There will be wonderful memories with special people, where love and peace abound. And there will also be other seasons: of pain, of grief, and times where much forgiveness is needed. There will be circumstances that we must let go of, and people we must face who have hurt and disappointed us deeply. You will face times when God is doing a great work of planting things deep within you, and times where the growth and harvest have surpassed your wildest dreams. Some of these seasons are glorious, and some are very painful, but no matter the season, we all have to make the ongoing choice that in spite of what we encounter, God will always get our "yes".

CHAPTER 3

From mercy

Whenever we think of Christ, we should recall the love that led Him to bestow on us so many graces and favors, and also the great love God showed in giving us in Christ a pledge of His love; for love calls for love in return. Let us strive to keep this always before our eyes and to rouse ourselves to love Him.

Saint Teresa of Avila

I urge you, brothers and sisters, in view of God's mercy...

(Romans 12:1)

I am a water person. I love the beach, I love lakes, and in particular I love the Colorado River. Anything with water does my soul good, and whenever I have time off I try to get some rest by the pool or by heading to the beach. Water has always been a part of our family's life as well; one of our favorite things to do is to go to the Colorado River and just check out for a week or two, as it's a great place to boat with the kids. But when summer arrives we are always at the beach. There is nothing like southern California's beaches, and one of the great things about the beach is that you can play or do nothing, and both are equally restful. However, there is one day in particular I will never forget.

My son, John, was quite young and he had walked down to the water, as he had a thousand times before, and I was watching him, as I had a thousand times before. I remember as I briefly turned my head to say something to my friend, in a split second I saw my John get swept into the ocean by a wave. I jumped out of my chair and started running, along with my daughter Camie Rose who is older than John, diving into the water, losing my nice sunglasses, and trying desperately to reach him. Every time I got closer, another wave would grab him and he would be taken out farther. John started to panic, and when I saw that, I started to panic; my daughter was screaming and it felt like a nightmare was happening in slow motion. My John was in trouble. I remember the moment when I knew I couldn't get to him.

I was praying, or more like scream-praying, and all of a sudden from the ocean's side, a man came out of nowhere, swept John up in his arms, and brought him to the shore. We were crying, we were all shaking, and I was nauseous. I remember turning around to thank the man, but we couldn't find him. As my friend went to yell at the young lifeguard, who was flirting with some girls and had negligently failed to see my drowning boy, I held on to John so tight I probably scared him even more. Later that day, I took John's hand and slowly walked him down to the water. I knew if he didn't feel the water on his toes and have me bring him comfort at the same time, he might never return to the water again.

The next day, still a bit shaken by the whole event, I began praying, really in gratitude for the Lord sending that man from nowhere to rescue my boy. I felt the Lord tell me that what happened with John is exactly what happens when sin overtakes our lives. Just like losing John in that brief moment happened so fast, sin, if empowered, has the ability to sweep us away. No one begins life hoping to get addicted and lose their family, and no one plans to end up in bondage.

NONE OF US WOULD SAY "YES" TO SIN IF WE SAW THE BIGGER PICTURE OF THE DAMAGE IT CAUSES. THERE IS ALWAYS FREE CHEESE IN A MOUSETRAP AND THE ENEMY OFTEN USES THE MOST ENTICING OF WAYS IN ORDER TO GET US TO REACH FOR WHAT LOOKS APPETIZING.

The enemy is a thief; he's not a robber. He is subtle and sneaky, and before we know it, just standing at the shore of sin – only playing in the shallow area – every small step sucks us into deeper water, and before we realize it we have been swept out beyond our control. Sometimes we feel stupid for making poor choices that took us to a place we never thought we'd ever be. How many times have we looked back at our lives, wondering, "Why did I say 'yes' to this, why did I give in to that temptation, why wasn't I wiser, why didn't I use more safety measures?"?

Sadly, that's what sin does. It doesn't play nice and it doesn't play fair. Any area where we just slightly yield by giving ourselves to its power, we can so easily be taken out to the point where we have lost all direction and control to be able to come back to the shore. Empowerment works both ways; it's either more of God, or more of something else. When we empower the "something else",

God is more than able to rescue us, as He did my boy John, but how He rescues us is often different to how we think He will.

Although I believe it was probably an angel that saved my boy that day, I was quickly reminded that I couldn't take my eyes off of John, not even for a moment. From that day I was even more careful every time John went near the water. No matter how God sends us a way out, we still have a responsibility to become wise and make the needed changes so we don't get taken in again. Precautions over our own hearts have to be non-negotiable. We easily forget just how sneaky the enemy is, and a moment of weakness can hurt us deeply. I don't mean that we should be paranoid, but wisdom can save us much hardship.

A few years back I was doing several conferences in New Zealand and I had a rare morning off. New Zealand is stunning in beauty with an old English-style charm of architecture, small village-type settings, and some of the most beautiful beaches, with rolling, green hills and sheep wandering; it's very picturesque. Walking along the beach, I felt I heard the Lord say, "Christy, you need to be careful, as the enemy is in no hurry to get you."

Do you know that the enemy is in no hurry to get you? I wasn't aware of any blatant sin in my life at the time when I was having this chat with the Lord, yet I felt what He said was so clear that I wrote it down quickly in a book I was reading.

The truth is, there is a real enemy; his tactics are sneaky, and his offers enticing. One of my pet peeves is when someone says sin isn't fun. Of course sin is fun! If it wasn't, we would never give in to it. Sin is always fun for a season. But when the season ends the destruction can be great.

THE ENEMY IS IN NO HURRY TO GET YOU; THE ENEMY IS IN NO HURRY TO GET ANY OF US, AND NO ONE IS ABOVE GETTING CAUGHT.

His plan is to get and keep us separated from God, and destroy every part of our life. His goal and his tactics are consistent, and many times God warns us to be wise; even stepping into the shallow waters can easily take us to a place no one wants to end up.

Not one of us is above any sin. Sin and separation from God are always lurking around the corner, trying to seduce us; **the seduction might come in different ways for each of us, but no one is above being seduced.** Separation is often a slow process. In fact, I hate that expression the church uses: "when someone falls". Although I do believe we're all one step away from stupid, no one ever just falls; it is never an overnight choice. It's often several smaller choices where the enemy's temptation to "stick our toes into the shallow end" seemed harmless.

You might be at a point in your life where you feel like you're way out in the sea, pulled in every direction, with no hope of coming ashore. Or you may be in a place where you know there are a few areas in your life that need to change. No matter where you're at today, change is always possible; as long as you have breath, God has the power to restore and redeem any area of your life. However, we don't start by trying to fix everything that we know needs changing, especially our behavior. Changing our lives never begins with behavior; change begins with how we think.

A healthy walk with God, how we see ourselves, how we love and interact with others, our relationships, and all those things that matter most, each begins with our thought life. However, before we can talk about our thought life, we have to first talk about who our God is. If we don't know who God is, we'll never trust Him, and if we don't trust, we won't yield. My son John had to trust me to take him down to the water again– the place that was terrifying had to be faced, but he had to trust that I would protect him. John was scared, but he went along, knowing Mommy would make sure he was OK.

I shared in the beginning that our choices of yielding to God are a must in order to have real change in our lives. This isn't about our willpower; this is about surrendering our mind to come under submission to Jesus. Where our mind goes is where we go. What has your mind is what has you. So ask yourself: What has my mind?

You can't think one way and live another. How we think is how we then behave. That's the way that God has set life up, yet too much of the time we do this in reverse! We often try to stop certain behavior, and change the way we interact with God and others, but we never fix our thinking. Attending conferences, or hearing what we need to change, isn't what changes us. If that was true, then the entire world would be different. If every person who attended church or a Christian event, just in the last year, went back home and implemented everything that was taught, then our world would not be in the condition it is today. There seems to be a huge disconnect between what we hear and what we live. James writes, "don't just listen to God's word. You must do what it says" (James 1:22 NLT). It's not just what we hear that's important – it's what we do with it that matters.

Maybe you're like me and you're unaware of some things that need to change in your life. Or perhaps you are fully aware of what needs to change, but you've chosen to ignore them, hoping they will just go away. Or perhaps you're so frustrated with yourself in certain areas because you know what needs to change, but you don't know where to begin. In our journey with God, He often leads us to places we find uncomfortable, even terrifying, but He does so to reveal things at the right time; no sooner and no later. When God leads and reveals, He also gives us the grace to walk through whatever we're seeing, encountering, or feeling.

Turning on the lights

Often when God begins to reveal things to us, it's like a light bulb goes on within us. We begin to see things that maybe we didn't before. We all have areas that need God's light, and even though they may be visible to others, it is not until He chooses to reveal those things to us that we're able to see them clearly. But God's timing is His for a reason, and when His light comes to reveal, His power is also present to heal.

One day I was reading about a carpet-cleaning business that was offering a special service for removing pet urine odors. They were offering free demonstrations to the customers to give them an idea of why they should buy the service. They explained that in the process they darken the room and then turn on a powerful black light. The black light causes urine crystals to glow brightly. Once the light comes on, every drop can be seen, not only on the carpet, but also on walls, drapes, furniture, and even on lampshades. Often when the customer sees the filth that they're living in, they don't care what it costs; they just want it cleaned up. Now the stains were there all the time, but they were invisible until the right light exposed them. We all have areas in our lives where we are totally unaware of just how much staining there is. We all have places that need to be cleaned up, but sometimes we are unable to see where they are. It's not until the light comes in that we can see them clearly. However, the problem isn't revealed just for revealing's sake, that would be cruel; instead **God shines the light of His holiness on the blackness of our hearts, not to make us feel guilty but rather to lead us into healing.**

The Spirit of God, who reveals and convicts, also has the power to cleanse, heal, and change us. When God shines His light into areas of our lives, He is always faithful to walk it through with us. In fact, if God is revealing something to you that needs changing, it means that what you're living in right now is less than what He has in mind for you. Something better is waiting. It takes God's leading, but it also takes His power, both to reveal and to heal. God doesn't show you the stains in your life to discourage, but rather to encourage you for greater things. Benjamin Franklin once stated: "How few there are who have courage enough to own their faults, or resolution enough to mend them!"

God's grace is a by-product of Him revealing the areas where we need healing.

THE WORST THING WE CAN DO WHEN AN AREA OF WEAKNESS IS EXPOSED IS TO IGNORE IT, PLAY LIKE WE DIDN'T HEAR IT, OR TRY TO FIX IT ALL AT ONCE WITH OUR OWN POWER.

When I took my John back to the water that day, he had to trust that what Mommy was doing was best, and even though to his limited understanding it would have felt a bit like torture, it was actually mercy. It was an act of mercy, knowing that if we did not push past the initial shock and pain of what he went through, John could always have a fear of water. Mercy doesn't always feel like mercy, yet just as John trusted me, we have to trust God, that wherever He is leading, it is always for the best. It is the sovereignty of God which reveals His mercy to us.

Think about where your life was before you knew God. The state we were in before we met Him was far worse than anything we find ourselves in now. Without mercy there is no hope, no future, and nothing to live for. But with mercy, we not only find hope, we also find the will of God and purpose for our lives.

Paul's reality

Paul writes from experience. He knows the mercy of God is everything, because it was everything to him. Paul "urges" us, which means to plead or to beg. He knows that if we live from this place then we can live out the "why" of our own lives. Paul was ambushed by the mercy of God to such an extent that he never recovered, and never forgot it:

> Even though I was once a blasphemer and a persecutor
> and a violent man, I was shown mercy because I acted in
> ignorance and unbelief [...] But for that very reason I was
> shown mercy so that in me, the worst of sinners, Christ Jesus
> might display His immense patience as an example for those
> who would believe in Him and receive eternal life.
>
> (1 Timothy 1:13, 16)

Before encountering God, Paul (then called Saul) had persecuted Christians, holding the coats while he watched them being stoned to death. He haunted, taunted, and destroyed those who put their faith in Christ. As the church feared Paul, and prayed against him, the Lord set His mercy towards him. Christ stooped low to get his attention, to have mercy on him, to give him a chance. And Paul never forgot it. This is who Jesus is.

Situations that we have prayed would go away, and people that we have prayed against, God has His eyes set to redeem. As my friend Simon Ponsonby says, "Only God can take a murderer and turn him into a martyr." That's the power and the mercy of the gospel message. There is nothing more powerful, and nothing more merciful, than the gospel. God comes down to us, and for us. We are the object of His coming.

The change in Paul's life was so drastic and dramatic that still today we learn from his words, his faith, and his example. History is full of examples of people who lived with eternity in mind. Paul was one of those. He is marked as one of the 100 most influential people of all time. Now that is influence! Yet, even with all of Paul's influence, he always refers to himself as "a servant of Christ". How many have done much less, but consider themselves as so much more? Yet here we find Paul – who was high up within the Jewish religion, who had an educated and influential background, who ended up writing much of the Bible, who forged the way for the church and saw many miracles and people coming to know Jesus – this Paul, still referring to himself as a servant. I wonder if one of the reasons that we can go off course in life, especially in ministry and church life, is because we work our way out of this servant call. With all the distractions of titles, positions, and anointing, have we forgotten that our highest call is to be a servant of Christ?

> WE DON'T WORK OUR WAY FROM THE PLACE OF SERVANT TO HIERARCHY, BUT RATHER FROM SERVANTHOOD TO SERVANTHOOD. THE TITLE MIGHT CHANGE, BUT THE POSITION NEVER DOES. OUR HIGHEST POSITION IS ALWAYS AS A SERVANT.

Paul understood that it was the mercy of God that saved him, and also the mercy of God that allowed him to become a servant. Being a servant isn't a role to disdain, but rather a privilege to be celebrated. It is an honor to receive the invitation to serve, and that's what Paul modelled; he always saw what he did as a privilege, not a pain. It can be easy to view our lives, and even some of the things we do for God, as a pain; everyday problems, other people, and life itself all have their difficulties, but as Paul teaches us time and time again, serving God is always a privilege. I often need to remind myself of this. If we forget the privilege of the call, we become overcome by the pain of it all. We don't have to do what we do; we get to do what we do. We are not trapped by people, calling, ministry, or the church; instead it is the mercy of God which invites us to see the bigger picture; encountering mercy brings a new perspective on everything.

I know that many people feel trapped, because I often hear from those who feel like there is no way out of their situation. I hear this often from church leaders who feel that if they don't keep serving in what they are doing, then their church will fall apart. In fact, you might be reading this right now, feeling that you are trapped in a relationship, a behavior pattern, an addiction, or even a ministry assignment. But the good news is that there is a way out. Mercy reminds us that it is God alone who holds everything we do, whether it is our marriage, the ministry, or things we struggle with. When God enters, His mercy enters, and it can take our Saul situations and turn them into Paul ones. Mercy changes everything.

When the apostle Paul suffered excruciating pain, the "thorn in my flesh" (2 Corinthians 12:7), I am sure he was hoping God would just remove the pain. When we're in pain and cry out to God, what we're often saying is, "God, please change this! Get rid of this pain!" Paul says, "three times I pleaded with the Lord to take it away from me" (verse 8), yet God didn't. Instead, He chose to give Paul what he needed to get through it. This is grace being walked out. **Often we feel that God is ignoring us if He's not removing what's painful,** yet we are never left alone. Instead we have the promise of His grace. His grace is always sufficient and gives us the power to be content. Personally, I would much rather have God change me in an instant, or remove what's difficult, than give me grace, but it's not usually the way He works. Grace gives us just enough to walk through whatever challenges we have to deal with today.

IF GOD IS NOT CHANGING YOUR CIRCUMSTANCES, IT'S BEST TO JUST ASK FOR STRENGTH AND POWER — TO NOT ONLY WALK THROUGH THEM, BUT TO LEARN FROM THEM.

If God isn't changing our season, then we need to find out why, instead of looking for a way out, or a quicker route. Is there anything we are missing? We don't often see the areas of growth that need to take place in us. One of the gifts of mercy is God's grace to empower us to stay.

WE NEED THE MERCY OF GOD TO FACE THE THINGS IN US THAT NEED TO CHANGE. MERCY MUST ALWAYS START WITH US.

I have realized that when I am in a season facing things I would rather avoid, I must not over-think what's happening, or try to figure everything out, but rather focus my energy in looking to, and surrendering to, Jesus.

Where is God at work? Hearing God in these times is vital to our growth. One of the scariest, but most productive, prayers is to ask God what is wrong with you. He will answer your prayer! The Lord is ever so faithful to speak to us, guiding us into what He is doing, but these times also reveal it is equally important to have the right people around us as well. We need mercy towards ourselves, but we also need mercy from people who love and are for us, and who will also confirm God's work in our lives.

Waiting for God, and receiving confirmation about what He may be doing, is God's gift of provision to us. So many things get messy because we're trying to change something the Lord isn't initiating. In other words, we see something about ourselves that we don't like, and get so self-focused in trying to change that we can't think about anything else. Or someone around us wants us to change, so they force us into a season to look at something we're not ready for. When God brings things up, He always gives us the grace and mercy to deal with them.

WHEN CHANGE IS FORCED BY OTHERS — WHEN IT'S NOT GOD, BUT RATHER THEIR DESIRE TO SEE US CHANGE — IT CAN CREATE CHAOS WITHIN US. THE CHANGE COULD ACTUALLY BE NEEDED, BUT IF A PERSON OTHER THAN THE HOLY SPIRIT IS INITIATING THE CHANGE, THEN THE MERCY THAT'S NEEDED IS MISSING. CHANGE WITHOUT MERCY IS EXHAUSTING.

It's good to remember that what people do with their life is up to them. Each of us carries our own convictions. Convictions are personal, not universal.

WE ARE NOT THE HOLY SPIRIT FOR OTHER PEOPLE. IT IS NOT OUR JOB TO FIX PEOPLE, GET THEM TO THINK LIKE US OR ACT LIKE US; IT IS OUR ROLE TO LOVE, EVEN IN DISAGREEMENT.

Otherwise, even with good intentions, we can easily cause a distance in the relationship when we try to fix people and resolve their issues. Even if our intentions are loving, we can come across as judgmental. Every one of us has been judged in different ways, and it's not enjoyable. Have you ever enjoyed being judged? I've never once been really grateful for judgmental opinions that people have had about my life, and never once has it convinced me to change.

Even in the church, we put religious language on things so we can manipulate people into change. We use the word "opinion", saying things like, "this is just my opinion", or "this is what God has been leading me to tell you…"

OPINIONS ARE OFTEN JUDGMENTS IN DISGUISE AND THEY CAN DO A LOT OF DAMAGE; THEY CAN EASILY RUN OVER PEOPLE'S FEELINGS AS IF THEY DON'T EXIST.

In fact, some of you have never recovered from the "opinions" that other people have had over your life. They've been stumbling blocks that you can't seem to get rid of, and every time you try to change they are quick to make you feel that you're "less than" others.

Mercy without judgment

Sometimes when I think about what people have said to me through the years, I just have to laugh, although much of it was not funny at the time. I know what it feels like to hear people's opinions and criticism, whether to my face or behind my back; I have caught the whispers of people's opinions about what I wear, how I lead, or even why I should get to lead. You cannot be in leadership of any kind and not live with some level of criticism. I found that out quickly living in Orange County, CA, where women in leadership are scarce; being in head church leadership gains its own congregation of judgment. Everyone has an opinion.

We all have these well-wishers in our lives. The hardest part about having critics is discovering who they are. Sadly, most of our harshest critics are people we would never expect it from.

IT'S IMPORTANT NOT TO ALLOW WHO THE CRITICISM COMES FROM TO DIVERT YOU FROM WHAT GOD'S DOING IN YOU.

Judgment is always near, always lurking, waiting to discourage, discredit, and damage all of us from saying "yes" to God's leading.

You cannot have change without some form of criticism either. Even with the best of intentions, not everyone will want you to change what you're doing, or who you are, because if you change, it will force them to look at their own lives, and not everyone wants to look in the mirror. To be honest, criticism that I have received has not been my main concern; what bothers me more is to think about my own self-righteous judgments. I cringe to think that I myself have made people feel the weight of unfair judgment rather than lead them gently to the God of mercy. How easy it is to regret those things that were not led by the Spirit of God and have therefore led to separation and frustration.

The word for judgment in the New Testament comes from the word "krino" and it means to separate, so it's impossible for us to love and judge at the same time. Even with good intentions (or overly religious intentions), when judgment is present it separates us from those we would have liked to influence in positive ways. We've all done that, it's just that some are more intentional than others; manipulation in any form never lasts, but it often does a lot of damage, especially if the manipulation is spiritual.

IN MY OWN LIFE, JUDGMENT HAS NEVER BEEN THE DOORWAY TO FREEDOM. IT WAS LOVE WITHOUT ANY HINT OF JUDGMENT THAT DISARMED MY DETERMINATION TO PUT MY ARMOR ON. MERCY IS DISARMING.

It was love for no reason, and kindness without expectation, that allowed me to know more about the God I love, and to open myself to believe change was possible. If we think our judgments will help people get free, then we have placed ourselves in a position that God Himself has said is not our place. It is not our job. Now some people will read this and think that the church is judgmental, and then they look at the church and judge it.

JUDGMENT IS JUDGMENT. SO WHETHER IT IS TOWARDS THE CHURCH OR TOWARDS THE WORLD, IT'S NEVER RIGHT AND IT'S NEVER OUR PLACE, SO WE ARE NOT EVEN EQUIPPED TO DO IT PROPERLY.

The Bible clearly indicates what we are to judge rightly in leadership and in caring for the church – it is God's idea, and when done properly it always provides space for people to get well.

Having areas of change needed in my own life I have found that I don't have a problem admitting my weak areas to God. In fact, talking to God about my weaknesses has always been one of the most powerful things in my relationship with the Lord. One of my favorite things to do is just be with God and spend time in prayer, often praying for myself. However, choosing to share my struggles with others, who might reject, judge, or condemn me, has been a process – at times a long process. But God made it clear to me that a huge part of my healing would be through relationship.

Left alone we just don't do well. The mercy of God is often expressed through relationship, because He is an all-relational Father. The Bible says:

> Two are better than one, because they have a good return for their labor: If either of them falls down, one can help the other up. But pity anyone who falls and has no one to help them up. Also, if two lie down together, they will keep warm. But how can one keep warm alone? Though one may be overpowered, two can defend themselves. A cord of three strands is not quickly broken.
>
> (Ecclesiastes 4:9–12)

Healthy relationships have the power to pull us up when we feel as if we're drowning.

NO BROKEN PERSON CAN HEAL THEMSELVES ALONE. MUCH OF OUR HEALING COMES THROUGH THE PEOPLE THAT GOD SENDS INTO OUR LIVES.

Whether we like it or not, we will never be fully whole without healthy community. If you don't have a few people to journey through life with, ask God which community He has for you, and then join it. Don't over-think it! Over-thinking things often kills the risk-taker in us. As with all choices, stepping deeper into community is a risk. Anything that changes us for good has risk attached to it – that is just part of how it is. But admitting our needs to God is only a part of the healing process; some of our deepest healing will only be found in the relationships that God places around us.

There is not a person alive who isn't in need of mercy.

GOD IS MORE WILLING TO GIVE MERCY THAN WE ARE TO ASK FOR IT. I, MYSELF, AM A TESTIMONY OF WHERE JUDGMENT ONCE CAUSED SEPARATION, THE POWER OF LOVE AND MERCY ATTRACTED ME BACK INTO THE PURPOSES OF GOD.

But I have had to take a risk in the relationships God placed in my life. True mercy and love attract us to God and to God-like people, who create places of safety where honesty, without fear of judgment, is present. Where there is no judgment, truth can be present, and where truth is, freedom has the power to do its job.

What's so encouraging about Paul's words is that over and over, he tells us that it is OK to admit our struggles. It is godly to acknowledge our position in Christ as being a servant, who constantly needs to be filled, time and again, with much-needed mercy. Paul modelled to us that no matter our position, until we are with Jesus, we will need His grace to get there.

I have come to realize that I can have a lot of mercy for other people, yet I tend to be critical and judgmental towards myself. It has taken me a long time to realize that the expectations I held, and the feelings of being overly responsible for things, gave me no room to have mercy for myself. I love talking about mercy. I love seeing others encounter the mercy of God and seeing their lives redeemed, yet I was holding out for myself. I was not very good at being kind to myself. I had to work through the idea that it was OK to need more than I realized. Ask yourself if you are good at receiving mercy. How kind are you to yourself? Many people struggle with judging others, because they don't have mercy for themselves. We often redirect towards others what we may be lacking in ourselves. Oftentimes we're looking to others for things to change for us, when the truth is that change often starts from within. One of my favorite reminders is: "If you don't like something, change it. If you can't change it, change your attitude about it" (Maya Angelou).

Coming to the realization that I needed to be kinder to myself didn't happen out of thin air, it first had to be modelled to me. You may be someone who has never had much mercy extended to you so you wonder why you should give mercy to others. Many people think like this, as if mercy is a choice, but Christ says the opposite: "Blessed are the merciful, for they will be shown mercy" (Matthew 5:7). In other words, if you want mercy, you must first be a mercy giver. The word "blessed" here also means favor or happy. Choosing to show mercy is a happy thing! Have you ever met someone who is quick to judge? Have you also noticed just how unhappy they are as a person? It is an unhappy life for the one who is unmerciful.

Just as with anything else in God's kingdom, where we are lacking in an area, we must be intentional about taking the steps to go after it. If I find myself in a position of needing something, then

I make the choice to give it away myself. If I find myself needing friendship, I will go out of my way to meet up with various people. You don't have to look far; we are often surrounded by what you and I are in need of. In other words, if I am not being shown mercy, I will go out of my way to administer mercy. Mercy is needed everywhere in every relationship. More importantly, mercy is the way in which God operates: "Administer true justice; show mercy and compassion to one another" (Zechariah 7:9).

I would encourage those of you who have been hurt by the judgments of others, and where mercy may have been missing in your own life, to change it.

TAKE WHAT YOU WERE MISSING AND DECIDE YOU WILL NOT MAKE ANOTHER PERSON FEEL WHAT YOU YOURSELF HAVE WALKED THROUGH.

In doing this you are not only changing patterns, you are also sowing into mercy, which is rewarded by having mercy in return.

When I am struggling to be merciful, I remind myself of the words of Paul: "in view of God's mercy [...] offer your bodies as a living sacrifice" (Romans 12:1). The place of God's mercy is where we are to view and live our lives from. Remember, here in Romans 12 Paul is leading us into knowing the will of God for our lives. He is writing about purpose, and how we can know what to spend our lives on. Yet we cannot be on the right track without mercy leading the way.

Mercy is not just something we give and receive; mercy is something we are called by God to love. "He has shown you [...] what is good. And what does the Lord require of you? To act justly and to love mercy and to walk humbly with your God" (Micah

6:8). When we are quick to show love and mercy to ourselves, and others, it is a good sign that we are growing up in Jesus!

When I think of mercy in the way Paul encourages, it makes it much easier to give to others what I know I myself am in great need of. I know what a mess I came from and I know I am a massive work in progress. I am all too familiar with my own areas of brokenness to realize that without mercy my life just doesn't work. Think about your life. Think about where you've come from and the mercy God has shown to you. Do you remember where you were before God entered your life? How did you get to where you are today? How many times has God come through for you when no one or nothing else did? How many times has God saved you from yourself? Where would you be today without the mercy of God on your life? If you look back through your life you will find mercy surrounding every part of who you are, and where you have been. The mercy of God is too massive, and deep, and spiritual, for any of us to really understand, but without it we have nothing. The mercy of God is leading, protecting, and caring for us way more than we know!

A few years ago, I was in a situation that didn't make any sense to me. You know those times where you can't make sense of what's happening and at the same time you're wondering why this is happening to you or people you love? I felt that God hadn't protected me like He could have, and in my mind should have. I didn't understand why He had allowed a certain situation to happen, and honestly I was super frustrated with Him.

In the midst of my complaining I felt I heard the Lord say to me, "Christy, you have no idea what I protect you from." I remember just stopping, and thinking that through. I have no idea what God's protected me from. I was about to ask God to tell me what He had protected me from, but I stopped, because I quickly realized that I didn't really want to know! In sensing God's response to me, it was clear there were a lot of things going on above me, and around me, that I was completely unaware of, and if I knew all the details, I would quite likely be terrified and never want to leave the house again – so I left it at that!

It is the same for you. You may not think God has got your back, but the truth is God is doing much more than you realize. Have you ever thought about how many times God may have protected you when you were driving, or watched over you during an illness? How often has God protected your kids when they were at school, or playing at a friend's house? God has watched over and protected you, and those you love, more than you would ever want to know! His great mercy far exceeds the external things that we can see. Instead of focusing on what we think God isn't doing, and what we don't feel protected from, we must learn to redirect our focus to be thankful for the daily mercies that cover us, especially when we're totally unaware.

I remember asking the Lord one morning, "Why did You say that Your mercy is new every morning?" And I sensed the Lord say, "Because yesterday's mercy is already used up!"

This again is the provision of God. He is fully aware we will blow it enough today that our mercy tank has to be refilled for tomorrow. Mercy will be waiting for you when you wake up. You don't have to worry, or get your mind concerned with tomorrow; you just need to live in the mercy God has given you for today, and it will be sufficient.

In 1 Peter, Peter writes about God's mercy in purpose; the inheritance God has given to each of us, not only throughout eternity, but also for today. What I love about this verse is that it is Peter talking about the mercy of God. Peter, who I love because he was a risk-taker, and who also lacked social skills! Do you have a friend who you love, but every time they talk you get a little worried about what they might say? To me, that's who Peter was. He was a "foot-in-mouth" kind of guy, where you never knew what he would say or do. Prior to writing the letter of 1 Peter, he had blown it big time, having to walk through the greatest embarrassment of his life after denying Jesus three times. Imagine all of his feelings: not only of disappointment in himself, but also trying to figure out what the crucifixion of Jesus meant.

His thoughts must have been spinning, thinking about his own choices, and how he had failed someone he loved deeply. Peter didn't understand a lot, but one thing he knew: Jesus had great love and mercy towards him. "In His great mercy, He has given us new birth into a living hope through the resurrection of Jesus Christ from the dead, and into an inheritance that can never perish, spoil, or fade" (1 Peter 1:3–4).

Peter had experienced the great mercy, and the new hope, that he was speaking of.

WHEN WE ENCOUNTER GOD'S MERCY IT ALWAYS REVIVES OUR HOPE FOR OUR FUTURE. THE MERCY OF GOD WANTS TO LEAD YOU INTO THE PURPOSES OF GOD.

In this journey of transformation, God is never surprised, nor is He distant. No matter your failures, your embarrassments, or the areas in your life where you feel like nothing will ever change; God's mercy is right there waiting to heal you, and lead you deeper into purpose.

CHAPTER 4

Never take your worship hat off!

[This] is your spiritual worship

(Romans 12:1 ESV)

Everything in life begins and ends with worship; we are born to worship, and we will end by worshipping for eternity. And in between those times, worship is what we must learn to completely give ourselves to, in every area of our lives.

I f you ask five different people what worship is, you'll probably get five different answers. If you visit five different churches, you'll probably see five different expressions of worship.

I have always loved worship because I've always loved music, and I used to wish I was more musical – both my kids are musical but they sure didn't get that from me! Some of my fondest childhood memories are to do with worship, and as a child, one of my favorite things to do was to go to church at the Vineyard on Sunday nights to worship. We met in the old gymnasium at Canyon High School, in Anaheim Hills. My dad took us early to help him set up the chairs and roll out the carpet. It was so amazing to hear all those voices bouncing off the walls of the gym. I was just a kid so I didn't realize just how significant those times in church really were until later. Now that I look back I can see not only how special, but in its simplicity how pure the worship was. There was always prayer ministry taking place, and worship music playing in the background, so those two things have always gone hand in hand for me.

There is nothing like worship. One of my favorite things on the planet is to worship! So in the early days of the movement, when Vineyard Music and New Breed began to form from within Vineyard Ministries, it was a natural fit for me to become involved. Watching all that God did in forming the teams and the songs was something so sweet and a time that can never be recreated. There is something really sacred that happens in church before people realize what or how they can use it for their own gain. Thinking back, it's amazing how the songs went around the world and influenced the church at large without the technology of today, or the Internet! It could only have been a God thing.

Vineyard worship took off, but not because of the Vineyard, it was because of Jesus. Worship of course wasn't in itself new, but the style, the model, the intimacy, were new to us. Bands became a normal part of church life, and it was amazing to watch how people encountered Jesus in new ways through the intimacy and simplicity of worship. In fact, if you ask these people who experienced the Vineyard then, most would probably say that it was worship that changed their lives. It was something sacred before money and fame were involved. As I look back I can honestly say that there was purity to it, and purity cannot be faked.

I learned a lot from my father-in-law, John Wimber, particularly in the area of worship. "Worship", he would say, over and over, "is the one thing that belongs to God alone." When John said things like that, they carried a lot of weight, because he was visible in Christian circles, and when the Vineyard worship really took off, John lived what he preached; he wasn't tempted to make it about himself or his organization, it remained about God. One of the things I deeply admired about him was that he would not be bought. He had "made it" already as a writer for The Righteous Brothers, and selling out in terms of worship was never an option for him. There were many opportunities to gain money and visibility, but that was never his goal. We had numerous conversations about how to keep worship about Jesus, and about making sure that finances didn't become a drive. Lots of people say they would never be bought, but they've never experienced the temptation to know what it means to be able to make that statement.

WE ALL HAVE A BIT OF A JUDAS INCLINATION WITHIN US, AND IF WE'RE NOT CAREFUL WE CAN EASILY BE BOUGHT.

The trio of money, fame, and sex has taken out many gifted women and men in church leadership, including in the area of worship. Sadly, I have seen this many times over.

Prior to Vineyard Music, we had Mercy Publishing, which published the songs that were happening in the church. This was John's company, and was part of our family's inheritance. But one day John gathered us all together, and asked if we could give Mercy over to Vineyard, because it was making so much money, and he didn't want to pollute anything. The name of Jesus, and the reputation of what God was doing within the Vineyard, were too important, and John didn't want this to not look right. So that's what we did; we gave it away. Only God knows if that was right, but I guess if you're going to do anything, it's best to play it safe, and go with not accepting even the appearance of things not being up to par. I so admire that commitment, even more so now.

The power of worship

I feel really privileged to have the philosophy that "it's not about me" engrained deep within me when it comes to worship. Watching what took place back then, and seeing how things are now, it is clear there has been a lot of change.

In the last quarter of a century, worship has become so diverse, and so central to church activity, that it has almost taken itself on the road. Worship events, even worship tours, have become a normal part of Christian culture.

CALL ME "OLD SCHOOL", BUT I'VE NEVER QUITE UNDERSTOOD HEARING THE WORDS "WORSHIP" AND "TOUR" IN THE SAME SENTENCE.

But that's the power of worship, it has the ability to have a life of its own.

Worship reveals the power of music, and music reveals the power of worship. Our life is God's artwork; we are a masterpiece created by the Master, and when we worship, we come to life. This art is revealed through the power of our lives. I recently read a brilliant article by T. Bone Burnett, which was taken from a speech addressing the music industry. His words rang so true, not just about the music industry, but also about the power in how God has wired us as individuals. He said this:

> Art is a holy pursuit. Beneath the subatomic particle level, there are fibers that vibrate at different intensities. Different frequencies. Like violin strings. The physicists say that the particles we are able to see are the notes of the strings vibrating beneath them. If string theory is correct, then music is not only the way our brains work, as the neuroscientists have shown, but also, it is what we are made of, what everything is made of.

WE HAVE BEEN WIRED FOR EXPRESSION. MUSIC ALONE HAS THE POWER TO CAUSE US TO REMEMBER EVERYTHING OR FORGET EVERYTHING.

Just by hearing certain songs it can launch us into places of ecstasy or despair. As much effort as I put into preaching and teaching every week, I know that, for the most part, people will remember tit-bits here and there. If they hear a song, however, they are more likely to remember that than my sermon. We correlate music with different seasons in our life. Even if it was many years ago, just hearing a certain song can easily bring back memories from the past.

Over the last thirty years or so, when I have asked people what really moved them when they visited the Vineyard, they have always said it was the worship. Worship tugs within the deepest parts of us, and draws us into a place of intimacy and hope, that doesn't often happen through just teaching. Both are important, but the power of worship hits people in places they didn't even know existed. Martin Luther said, "Beautiful music is the art of the prophets that can calm the agitations of the soul; it is one of the most magnificent and delightful presents God has given us."

WORSHIP IS MORE THAN A MUSICAL EXPRESSION; IT IS AN INDICATOR OF WHAT YOUR LIFE IS ALL ABOUT.

Even though music has great power, it is only one expression of worship. Worship is more than what we say it is, or even how we think it should look. God creating the heavens and the earth is an expression of His worship; everything surrounds worship. Everything that you have been created to do is worship. Art in itself is an expression of worship, but so is hospitality, teaching, or cooking. All expressions from our Creator reveal the power of worship. Everything in life begins and ends with worship; we are born to worship, and we will end by worshipping for eternity. And in between those times, worship is what we must learn to completely give ourselves to, in every area of our lives.

It is important to gather corporately to worship, not only because we can publicly express our faith, love, and gratitude to God, but also because it feeds our private times of connecting with Him. God says, "Never will I leave you; never will I forsake you" (Hebrews 13:5), and this I believe is one of His greatest promises to us. We will never be abandoned. Jesus also says that "where two or three gather in my name, there am I with them" (Matthew 18:20). There are some things that take place in a corporate gathering which we don't experience just in private times of worship. Both are equally important; God is at work in both settings.

IF THE PRIVATE AREAS OF OUR LIFE AREN'T DIRECTED TO GOD IN WORSHIP,
IT NOT ONLY AFFECTS THE CHOICES THAT WE MAKE, BUT IT SPILLS INTO OUR
OUTWARD EXPRESSIONS OF WORSHIP AS WELL.

One empowers the other. If we feel disconnected from God in any way, we end up spending less and less time with Him. What begins to follow? Our priorities about how we spend our time begin to change. We are probably not in the place of wanting to be with other believers, and so the desire lessens.

The picture of worship is learning to give ourselves completely to God, whether it's in the private times of intimacy, or in the choices we're making, or in gathering with other believers; all of these expressions matter to our lifestyle of worship. In the last chapter Paul encouraged us from Romans 12:1 to view our lives from God's mercy. He gives us steps on how to walk out a life of mercy. Making daily decisions to live sacrificially, and choosing to live holy lives because we know it pleases Him – this is what it looks like for someone to truly worship God. Paul asks the question, "because of all He has done for you" (NLT), how can you not live sacrificially? God has had tremendous mercy on us, over and over again, so then how can we not reject the shallow and temporary enticements of this life? Powerfully, and convincingly, Paul argues, how can we say "no" to the one who said "yes" to us?

Yet we do say "no". Sometimes unknowingly, sometimes willingly, we crawl back off the altar and give ourselves to other things. Paul is trying to get us to see the importance of every choice we make. We often misdiagnose the root problems in our lives. Where we lack clarity to make decisions, to know God's will in a situation, or are frustrated by dealing with the same old patterns of addiction, it is often due to an area of our worship that has been misdirected.

IF YOU DON'T REDIRECT YOUR WORSHIP BACK TO HIM, THEN THE PATTERN OF BEHAVIOR THAT YOU ARE STUCK IN WILL NEVER CHANGE.

A problem with anger, addiction, sexual sin, gossip, rage, or bitterness cannot be empowered if you choose instead to give that part of your life to God: "God, I choose to forgive as my act of worship," "God, I ask for peace instead of revenge and bitterness," "As my act of worship, I entrust this person/situation to You… I choose to set my heart and mind on You as an act of surrender in worship."

Remember that any area of our mind that isn't in full submission to Christ in worship is an area that the enemy has power in. The power behind worship is so great that if worship is used for any purpose other than what it was made for, God will address it, in our own lives as well as in the life of the church.

So, what is it that Jesus says about worship?

The battle for worship

When it comes to corporate worship, there is a sobering example taken from Palm Sunday (or Selection Day as it would have been called then), when Jesus makes His triumphal entry into Jerusalem. Jesus looks down at the city that He loves, and begins to weep (Luke 19:41). The word "weep" is not used lightly; it literally means to sob, to wail, a gut-wrenching cry. Among all of the people cheering and partying, here we find the Savior is weeping. Weeping over what He sees, weeping over the condition of the Temple – weeping over the place of worship. Then Jesus heads straight to the Temple. He is no longer weeping. His weeping has turned to anger.

We have to know what causes our God to be angry. You don't overthrow something unless you have a bit of emotion in you. There are places in Scripture where it speaks of the feelings and emotions of God. There are things God loves and there are things God hates. When Jesus begins to confront, he is giving a command. It is not said in secret, nor is it said in a soft tone; Jesus is angry and He is commanding them to listen. The place of prayer and worship is being used for money making; a place for offering worship to God has become a place of selfishness. And Jesus is furious.

This reveals how sacred worship is, and because of this, the enemy has always put his full efforts into trying to steal it.

THE BATTLE FOR YOUR LIFE, THE BATTLE IN THE CHURCH, AND THE BATTLE IN OUR RELATIONSHIP WITH GOD, HAVE ALWAYS BEEN OVER WORSHIP.

Satan was the original worship leader of heaven but wanted the worship for himself. He was kicked out of heaven because he tried to take something that didn't belong to him. Jesus Himself said that He "saw Satan fall like lightning from heaven" (Luke 10:18). This is an incredibly strong visual which should cause any believer to cringe. Satan's self-focus, and desire to be worshipped, had him thrown out of heaven faster than it takes the time to blink.

IF WORSHIP HAS THE POWER TO TAKE SATAN OUT, IT CAN TAKE US OUT TOO.

The enemy wants to steal your worship; whether personally or corporately, the enemy loves to steal that which belongs to God alone. We often see people worshipping in church, and it seems that all is good, yet only God knows what worship is really taking place. Lots of people worship well outwardly, but if you dig a little deeper, their mind may be elsewhere. Remember, it was Jesus who said, "These people honor me with their lips, but their hearts are far from me" (Matthew 15:8). The mind has to submit in worship. **My thinking has to align itself with where I'm at, who I'm worshipping, and why I am worshipping.** Some days are easier than others. Why? Because it's a battlefield. Some days the battle to enter in and to experience more of God comes easy, and other days it feels like trudging through mud.

A few years ago when I was studying, I couldn't get my mind focused. It was so frustrating because I was trying to prepare a sermon about the presence of God, yet I wasn't feeling much, and I was super distracted. In the midst of the distraction, I felt the Lord say, "Christy, you need to be present in My presence." Hmm. Present in His presence. As I started to think it through, I realized that I have to make the choice to be aware, to experience the fullness of His presence. We have to breathe in the presence of God, for "in Him we live and move and have our being" (Acts 17:28). From this act of worship we can then focus on God, rather than on whatever else is going on.

ALL THROUGH HISTORY EVERY REVIVAL HAS BEEN USHERED IN BY WORSHIP. THINK ABOUT THAT. EVERY TIME GOD HAS DECIDED TO MOVE, HE HAS PLACED WORSHIP AT THE FOREFRONT OF WHAT HE HAS CHOSEN TO USHER IN.

It is worship which led the way. We also find in the Scriptures that worship led God's people into battle throughout the Old Testament.

The battle with worship in your own life is over who will get your attention, your affections, and the glory from your life. **The fight has always been over glory.** We are the greatest masterpieces in God's artwork. Your life is an expression of God's work – His creation and His art. The enemy does not want that expression of Christ in you, because it carries a hope to be revealed. The enemy will do whatever he can to shut that down in you, often by causing your worship to get distracted, or directed to other things. Distraction is one of the enemy's tactics to hinder us from worshipping God.

WE THINK IT WILL BE A MASSIVE ATTACK FROM THE DEVIL THAT WILL TAKE US OUT, WHEN THE TRUTH IS THAT IT IS OFTEN THE DISTRACTIONS OF AN OPTION-FILLED WORLD WHICH CAN SLOWLY DISTANCE US FROM WORSHIP.

The things we don't think will be distractions are often the things which distract us the most. When we worship corporately, how easy is it to get distracted? We start wondering if we have locked the house, put the trash out, we start making our grocery list, or thinking about work, or what we need to get done that week. It's the same with the distractions outside of church. We get busy with life; trying to keep up with work, managing the family or our social life, and daily activities become overwhelming and take up a lot of time in our minds.

Worship is not something to be defined by outward appearance, but it is the position of the heart.

WORSHIP IS AN ACT OF THE MIND BEFORE IT'S AN ACT OF THE WILL.

Our thinking has to be aligned to worship God; our mind must submit in worship, daily. One of the most powerful one-on-one times for me in worship is when I'm cleaning. I hate cleaning but it seems to be a time where my interactions with God produce a lot of insight for me personally.

Just as we see how worship has played a key role in history, so the forces against it, and the arguments over it, go way back. Jews and Samaritans argued about where the real place of worship should be, and even today, we continue to compare and debate which type of worship is right. Churches have always argued over why we worship, how we worship, and who should get to worship. But the crazy thing is that worship is not about us! Worship is about our God.

Worship culture

In the kingdom of God, everything is a gift; faith is a gift, salvation is a gift, spiritual and natural abilities are gifts, because we serve a generous God who loves to give His kids good things. But worship is not ours to take. Worship is the one thing that belongs to God alone.

However, this is hard to see in some of the worship culture of today. Stepping into churches and events, we often hear about the people leading, or how great the songs were, rather than about the One we came to worship. Don't get me wrong, I love worship leaders and I love worship songs, especially when they speak sound, solid theological statements about the glory of God, and I genuinely love and appreciate those who can capture in song what I need to say to my God, but I don't love these things more than the One I came to worship!

The effectiveness of worship often gets compared to how good the sound quality was, or the fashion and image of those on stage. It is not uncommon to find more media posts from worship leaders about what they're wearing, or who they had dinner with, than about God Himself. This is not only from those in worship ministry, but visible Christian leaders in general. I was at one event a few years ago, where they dedicated a whole video to the fact that they had 2 million Facebook followers. Is that really what we're after? Has that become the goal of our gatherings? Sometimes just getting past all the distractions surrounding worship these days is not only discouraging, but exhausting.

I am not against things being big (I prefer being part of a bigger church), nor am I against having millions of Facebook followers, because I also believe that healthy things grow. I am completely for all of these things, but **the confusing messages, and what qualifies as success in ministry, I see as damaging – not only to the church, but to the message she carries.** A. W. Tozer said: "Worship is no longer worship when it reflects the culture around us more than the Christ within us."

I have often wondered why the church believes that we have to be like the world in order to reach the world. Why would we measure our success in the church by what the world says is successful? I was at a Christmas "worship" night a few years back, as I wanted to support some of my friends who were a part of it. I loved what they did, as they were true to themselves, and the

Holy Spirit was really present. But the group that was hosting the event did some of the exact same things that I'd seen at a Coldplay concert. Well, I loved it when Coldplay did these things because it was an awesome expression of their creativity. But when this Christian group copied them, it was a huge turnoff.

Why couldn't they have come up with their own creativity? Were they thinking, "It was successful for Coldplay so it will be successful for us"? Do we really believe that we have to look like the culture in order to reach the culture? Is that what success looks like for the church? Do we have to settle for copying what works in the world's models? Who knows why this group felt they had to copy, but there are many ways in which the church copies the world – thinking it will look cool or will get the world's attention, when in fact **it's embarrassing that we feel we have to copy in order to be effective. Fitting into the culture to reach the culture works against the call of the church. We cannot influence something which we ourselves conform to. Whether it is in our own personal worship, or corporate worship, fitting in or being relevant has never been the point.**

Paul's encouragement is to not do it, don't conform to the world around you. So whether it be in the church, in relationship, in business, in family, or even in worship, don't do it. To conform is the easy way out. Paul's encouragement is to live not with a mindset of settling into what is offered, but rather to walk into any situation with a mindset of asking what God can transform. What can God transform in my marriage? What can God transform in how I do business? How does God want to transform the way we do worship? There is nothing in the kingdom of God which has to do with settling into what we've been confronted with, but rather it's an opportunity to bring about change that would only happen with the transforming power of Christ. There is an excellence in effort when it comes to seeing beyond the obvious.

Of course we should do things well, and we should do church events with excellence in mind. But we should also be true to ourselves, operating in the calling and creativity that God has given us.

SUCCESS IN GOD'S KINGDOM IS NOT ABOUT SIZE, AMOUNT OF INFLUENCE, OR MONEY. SUCCESS IN THE KINGDOM OF GOD IS ABOUT BEING OBEDIENT, AND STEWARDING WELL WHAT GOD HAS ENTRUSTED TO US. THE SIZE AND SCOPE OF THIS IS UP TO GOD.

I believe in excellence; not only should God get our best, but the church should offer excellence in what we do, especially in how we worship God with our lives. But excellence is not financial status, not about having more or being more, but rather about taking what God has entrusted us with, whether in the private or public arena, and there being no question that we are giving it our best!

We all have our own times when we are deeply affected by worship. For me, often my most powerful worship exchanges with Jesus have been in the car, or when a band has so little to draw from that the distractions are few, but the heart is so present in God that it completely changes the atmosphere. Regardless of the musicianship, it is the truth in worship that releases freedom. If you've been in church for any period of time, you will have seen that there are good musicians, and there are also those who aren't that great, but because their hearts are honest, God shows up. It's an amazing picture, that **sometimes what we see as valuable may**

not be what God views as the most important.

I have told my worship community for years, "We work with what we have, until we get what we want." What I'm saying is that we aren't going to waste time stressing, or trying to be something more than what we are right now. Let's take what we have and be faithful with it. Let's honor God by giving Him our best. If God gives us more, then great, we'll take it! But whether we have a lot or a little, God deserves His worship, and He deserves to get the best from His own.

This is why Jesus said that with entrustment comes much responsibility. When people see leaders on the stage, they assume that is what it looks like to be a successful follower of Jesus. It doesn't matter if you lead ten people or 10,000. Leaders model to other people what it looks like to follow.

SPIRITUAL LEADERS, WHETHER IN WORSHIP, TEACHING, OR LEADERSHIP MINISTRIES, ALL HAVE GREAT RESPONSIBILITY TO POINT PEOPLE TO JESUS. IF FOR ANY REASON THE FOCUS IS MISDIRECTED, THEN THE WORSHIP BECOMES MISDIRECTED.

I don't believe we have seen the lasting fruit of the seeds sown into this past decade yet. Seeds take time to grow and produce fruit, but it's obvious that some of the fruit is revealing an unhealthy focus on outward appearance.

An outward focus, as I mentioned in an earlier chapter, undermines the power of the local church. It feeds an illusion that bigger is better, more is where it's at, and if no one knows your name then what you're doing is insignificant. No church can compete with that type of model, and those who do, have to hire people just to keep up. You don't need a light show for a church of forty people! The temptation in this direction is clear, and it will continue as long as it gets fed.

I actually believe this is one of the reasons why God moves around a lot; why He is always at work in so many places around the world, some visible, but most not. With the temptation to make it about us, no one person, place, or entity would be able to host that which must be quickly directed to God.

C. S. Lewis said:

> A silly idea is current that good people do not know what temptation means. This is an obvious lie. Only those who try to resist temptation know how strong it is. After all, you find out the strength of the German army by fighting against it, not by giving in. You find out the strength of a wind by trying to walk against it, not by lying down.

The temptation to take that which doesn't belong to us is great. I know because I have my own struggles when I walk off a platform after being used by God. I have to continually say "no" to what doesn't belong to me. I also know myself well enough to know that if I leave any tiny part of me open to praise that isn't mine, I am not above claiming it.

THERE IS A DEEP NEED FOR AFFIRMATION WITHIN ALL OF US; IT IS NORMAL TO DESIRE AFFIRMATION, YET IT'S DEADLY TO BE LED BY IT, ESPECIALLY WHEN IT COMES TO MINISTRY.

Pride lurks on the doorstep of the church and at the doors of our hearts, and we must be aware of its power.

I don't believe that people deliberately set out to steal that which belongs to God. However, I do see that the inner drive for fame and recognition is alive and well today in the church. In traveling the world, often going from stage to stage, I am always trying to challenge myself, asking, "Would I still do what I do if I didn't get paid?" What if no one knew my name? Would I still serve God faithfully if no one ever knew about it?

There are many of you who serve the local church, and so perhaps you feel that what I'm saying doesn't affect or concern you. My encouragement is that it should concern you. Whether you struggle with it personally or not, we should all be praying for those who are out there in the public eye. Whoever God is entrusting today, we need to pray for, because we want them to do well. We want them to be good stewards of what they've been given. For the sake of Jesus, we must be praying for those who have a visible platform, because it is not an easy road.

The love story of worship

So, we've looked at the power of worship, and what upsets God when worship is misused or misdirected; but what kind of worship is God looking for?

John chapter 4 is one of my favorite stories about the ministry of Jesus, and it gives such insight into worship.

First, it shows us that God is not seeking worship, but worshippers. God does not struggle with who He is; He doesn't need to hear how well He is doing. In fact He doesn't even need our worship (the angels are continually worshipping before His throne). Jesus tells us that the Father seeks those who will worship Him in Spirit and in truth (John 4:23). Again, this is a picture of worship as a lifestyle. Worship is something we do, a choice that we make, but being a worshipper is an identity – it is who we are.

We have to choose to enter into what's already taking place. Worship is full of action in every way; worship is a verb! It is not about shouting or silence, about form or tradition, but an expression of the heart. To worship in truth means that nothing is hidden. There is honesty from deep within which is given outward expression.

When our hearts are centered in the right place open to hearing and seeing who we really are, then truth reigns in honesty. Freedom is the by-product of truth. True worship changes us. If nothing is changing then something is wrong.

Worship may begin in song, but it plays out into every area of our lives. In your own life, the battle for who and what you will worship is always present.

THE THINGS THAT YOU BATTLE WITH IN YOUR OWN HEART – THIS IS THE BATTLE FOR THE WORSHIP OF YOUR LIFE. ANY PART OF YOUR LIFE THAT IS NOT SURRENDERED IN WORSHIP AND GIVING GLORY TO GOD WILL BE AN OPEN AREA FOR THE ENEMY. JUST REMEMBER, WHERE THE BATTLE IS GREATEST IN YOUR LIFE IS WHERE THE PROMISE IS GREATER.

We find this earlier in John chapter 4 where Jesus encounters the Samaritan woman. This is a woman whose life is directed in the wrong purpose. She was not created to be what she has become, but she doesn't know any better. The story illustrates how the way in which we love, or judge, affects our worship. But remember,

Jesus is also looking for worshippers, which he mentions to her later in the chapter.

Jesus intentionally reached out to this woman, a woman who was considered to be unacceptable in that society, and particularly should have been disregarded by Jesus; not only was she a Samaritan, she was a woman, and not only was she a woman, she was a promiscuous woman. She had three strikes against her. She was fully aware of her place within society, which is why her shame led her to approach life where avoidance was easier; it was shame which led her to draw water from the well in the heat of the day, just to avoid other village women. She knew what people thought about her, said about her, and that they wouldn't want to be seen with her. She was liked by the men and disliked by women! I can just imagine the disdain, the gossip, even the jealousy towards this woman. Jesus said that she had previously had five husbands – in those days only a man could divorce a woman, so this means that she had been divorced five times; therefore she had been repeatedly rejected and kicked to the curb.

She was rejected by everyone, even those who used her body, yet she was chosen by Jesus. To me this is a love story, revealing the deep need within each person to be seen and loved, despite their sin. No matter where we come from, at the core of each person is the fundamental desire, or need, to be loved and wanted. I have many weaknesses, but when someone chooses to love me, even in spite of me, it causes my head to turn, it touches me deeply. It disarms me. All through the Gospels, we read about the kindness of Jesus disarming many.

WHEN WE ENCOUNTER JESUS, WE ARE FACED WITH THE TRUTH OF WHO WE ARE, AND THE CHOICES WE HAVE MADE; BUT TO BE SEEN IN ALL OUR MESS YET LOVED IS DISARMING.

Winston Churchill is credited with saying, "Men occasionally stumble over the truth, but most pick themselves up and hurry off as if nothing has happened." Notice that not only did Jesus not reject her and all her baggage, but she also didn't run away. Sometimes we feel it is easier, especially when faced with truth, to shake it off and move on. But this Samaritan woman chose to stay, even when facing some very hard truths. **Encountering Jesus is to encounter not only the truth of who we are, but also the deeper desire within us, that we long to be loved even though it means revealing parts of us we would rather avoid. The need within us to stay is stronger than the desire to flee, even though it means the possibility of seeing things about ourselves that we hate.**

In verse 10, Jesus told her, "If you knew the gift of God and who [I am] ..." In other words, she didn't know there was another option. Jesus was there offering her the better option. He says the same to us today; if we knew the gift of Himself, of His presence, we wouldn't be wasting our time running after this or that, giving our worship to other things. Instead we would find our satisfaction in Him.

The way Jesus ministers to her shows much of who our Jesus is. He is so gentle with her, even while speaking hard truths. He doesn't try to sell her anything, he doesn't make her look stupid, or talk about how great He is to know everything while she knows nothing. Instead, He lowers Himself; He asks her for a drink.

This is a picture of servant love. This is how the King operates in His kingdom, lowering Himself, taking on the role of servant for the sake of another. To be successful in the world we have to sell ourselves, but in God's kingdom it's the opposite. We never hear Jesus brag or boast, and we never find Jesus using anyone for personal gain to build His ministry. Instead, He chose the route of servanthood.

In fact, Philippians 2:7 tells us: "He made himself nothing by taking the very nature of a servant." He chose to make Himself nothing for our sake. Just the thought of the King of Kings choosing to lower Himself so I can understand the message of who He is astounds me. This is why the power of leadership in Jesus' kingdom is all about servanthood. In fact, I can tell how my worship life is by how I am serving. How you and I serve reveals what we understand of kingdom leadership and servanthood.

Jesus says: "whoever drinks the water I give them will never thirst" (John 4:14). "Whoever" means that there is more than one drink available and it is for anyone. You and I are made to thirst and made to be filled, but there is only one way to satisfy the deepest thirst within us. Not every drink satisfies or quenches. If we drink and are still thirsty, then we are drinking from the wrong source.

When we drink from the right well, from Christ, it not only satisfies, but also reveals the counterfeit: places where we've settled for things that never truly satisfy. We will not be able to identify the counterfeit until we taste the real. The Bible tells us to, "Taste and see that the Lord is good" (Psalm 34:8). To taste of the Lord is to ruin our appetite for anything less. Once you have encountered Jesus, nothing else compares. When bankers are trained to recognize counterfeit notes, they need to become very familiar with the real notes so they can tell the difference.

SOMETIMES PEOPLE ARE SO USED TO LIVING WITH THE COUNTERFEIT IN THEIR LIVES THAT THEY DON'T EVEN KNOW WHAT REAL SATISFACTION IS. SO OFTEN PEOPLE ARE DRINKING FROM THE GUTTER, WHEN GOD IS SAYING, "I WILL GIVE YOU WATER FROM HEAVEN."

If you are not satisfied with your life – your marriage, your relationships, or your work life – then ask yourself what source you are drawing from. Where is your worship directed in these areas of your life? If you have been counting on any of these things to fulfil the deep needs within you, then you will never be satisfied. Until you redirect your worship to have those needs met by Him, you may end up frustrated, and even living in shame.

When Jesus addresses the counterfeit in the Samaritan woman's life, He is touching on her deepest heartaches. This would not have been easy to hear, yet she stays.

WHEN GOD BEGINS TO REVEAL AREAS OF OUR LIFE WHERE WE HAVE TRIED TO DRAW FROM THE WRONG SOURCE, IT IS OFTEN PAINFUL AND EMBARRASSING.

Jesus says to her, "Go, call your husband and come back" (John 4:16). Now her disguise begins to unravel, perhaps she is starting to see herself for the first time. Remember, she doesn't even know about another option, another way of living, another way to worship with her body rather than what she is currently using it for. She tells Him, "I have no husband" (verse 17), and He replies, "The fact is, you have had five husbands, and the man you now have is not your husband" (verse 18). What Jesus is saying is that He sees her; He understands that she has been rejected over and over, and that her current man is not even dignifying her enough to marry her. This is what happens when we come into contact with God. His light shines in us, and on us, and reveals the truth.

IT IS IMPOSSIBLE TO BE IN THE PRESENCE OF GOD AND PRETEND THAT EVERYTHING IS FINE, ESPECIALLY IF IT'S NOT.

The things Jesus is pointing out are hard truths, yet she doesn't run. Why didn't she run away from Him? Personally, I think it was because Jesus not only revealed the truth about her life, but also completely accepted her at the same time. Truth was wrapped in grace. This is our model, the perfect picture of what it looks like to interact with others, but also to face the truth within ourselves. One of my favorite things about Jesus is that He had an amazing way of looking past the sin and seeing the person. He speaks right to the need of this woman's heart, to show her that her value is much more than she realizes. It's so very loving. And even though her choices have led her to the wrong things, Jesus shows her that she has great value.

THERE IS NOTHING MORE POWERFUL THAN WHEN SOMEONE COMES ALONGSIDE US AND BELIEVES IN US BEFORE WE EVEN BELIEVE IN OURSELVES.

Jesus also speaks into the direction of her life, in essence saying, "Woman, you have been made to be a worshipper, and the torment of your life is that your life is misdirected, because your worship has been misdirected."

JESUS IS NOT ONLY SEEING, ACCEPTING, AND LOVING HER; HE IS ALSO
POINTING HER INTO HER PURPOSE.

Psalm 107:8–9 says, "Give thanks to the Lord for His unfailing love and His wonderful deeds for mankind, for He satisfies the thirsty and fills the hungry with good things," but do you know what it says before this? We are made to be fed and to have our deep needs met by God. We all have these needs, but if they aren't met by God, we will begin to fill them with other things. We must look at how we fill the needs in our lives.

Then ask yourself, are the choices you make revealing how truly valuable you are? Are the decisions you're making, and the time you're spending, showing the value that God speaks over your life? Or are you selling yourself short in certain areas? Are you trying to fill those spaces with counterfeit options? One of the many reasons why I love this story is that it's such a great and encouraging reminder that no matter how troubled we are, or how much baggage we may have, we can never change God's mind about our value.

When we realize we need help, God says: "Turn to Me, and I will fill those needs in you." Instead of trying to resolve, fix, or fill the need on our own, when we turn to God we are in fact saying, "You are the One I trust, and You are the One who knows how to fulfil my needs." This is your spiritual act, your spiritual choice to worship God. When we understand that it is God who fixes us, gratitude begins to stir within us.

A lifestyle of worship

Cooking is one of the things I love to do when I have time at home. When my kids were growing up, every Monday we had "new recipe night" when I would cook something new and the family would judge it. They were very honest, and still are, about what they like or don't like. In preparing for cooking, I learned years ago never to go grocery shopping when I'm hungry. Every time I shop when I'm hungry, I buy all kinds of things I don't like, let alone need. This is often a picture of what it looks like when we have areas of our lives that aren't met by God. The hunger was created by God, to be filled by God. When we worship things other than God it leaves emptiness inside. This emptiness often creates a hunger which causes us to panic and search to fill it with other things. If the hunger within us is not met by God, then we will settle for other things that only hurt our relationship with God, and often other people too. Those areas within us have to be made right; they have to be met by the only One who can fill those spaces within us. This is what it looks like to redirect our worship.

So if we are made to worship and it's the highest call of our lives, then we must treat worship not as a visitation, but a lifestyle. Worship is in the choices we make, each and every day of our lives. It has to do with how we spend our time, our money, and our energy. Whether our circumstances are joyful or difficult does not make God more or less worthy of our worship. He is always worthy, and one of the greatest expressions of our love is that we choose to worship, no matter what is happening in our life; that is one of the most amazing gifts we have to give back to God.

A few years ago I heard someone say, "If all else fails, worship." It bugged me when I heard that because I thought that's not right – instead, we should worship so that nothing will fail! I have a personal motto: "Worship, and say it until you believe it." Never take your worship hat off, because this is your life, your "yes" to Jesus! It's when we take our worship hat off, or misdirect our worship to other places, that we make a mess of our lives. There is no better time to worship than when our focus needs to be directed back towards God.

That's what Paul is saying in Romans 12:1 when he refers to the place of mercy. From the place of mercy, we throw ourselves on the altar of worship. Don't think of the altar as something you see at church, but rather look at the altar as if you are looking to your God. When you remind yourself of the mercy God has had on your life, those times He came through when no one or nothing else did, where His faithfulness filled you once again with hope, how can you then not worship? Out of those encounters with God's mercy, our worship flows as a natural response.

JUST AS GROWTH IS A BY-PRODUCT OF CHANGE, WORSHIP IS A BY-PRODUCT WHEN WE RECOGNIZE GOD'S MERCY IN OUR LIVES.

Worship is not some sort of "extra" – it comes from a deep place of gratitude that God would send His mercies anew to us every morning. To wake up to mercy is to respond in worship.

What does a worshipper do? What does a worshipper look like?

A worshipper of God is one who lives sacrificially: "offer your bodies as a living sacrifice […] this is your true and proper worship" (Romans 12:1). The word "offer" here means to present, to provide, to be near, and one of my favorites, to be at one's disposal (Blue Letter Bible).

This reminds us that our lives are not our own. We are at the disposal of another. Their best interest now becomes our best interest. Sacrificial worship is when your life is lived before God, and no matter the cost to you personally, you will stand your ground. You will make yourself available. To sacrifice is a choice, just as worship is a choice. A "living sacrifice" means it has the ability to move – either towards the altar of God, or towards the worship of other things. Our worship is always moving; but we must be aware what it is moving towards.

Getting our eyes off ourselves is the first step of surrender in worship, and it allows the sovereign One to take center stage in our lives. Introspection will always kill our worship. It's not about who we are, what we've accomplished, or even where we may have gone wrong, but it's all about who our God is. His great love and mercy to us are what enable us to offer our sacrifice out of gratitude rather than obligation. A loved person always wants to love in return, no matter the cost.

Sometimes worship is a sacrifice because we are making the choice to do something whether we feel like it or not.

THE SACRIFICE WE ARE WILLING TO MAKE FOR ANYTHING IN OUR LIVES REVEALS THE VALUE WE'VE PLACED UPON WHAT WE WANT. SACRIFICE IS A BY-PRODUCT OF WHAT WE TRULY SEE AS VALUABLE.

Some of the most valuable things are left untouched, or unfought for, as the price is too costly. Worship is costly. Worship involves sacrifice. Eventually you and I have to say "no" to other things if we truly want to be a living sacrifice, sold out for God. King David said, "I will not sacrifice to the Lord my God burnt offerings that cost me nothing" (2 Samuel 24:24). While we can't make His presence happen, we can prevent it.

We are willing to fight for those things that matter the most to us. Sometimes the greatest battle is over the self, the death of our ego in admitting our places of failure. The death to self is often one of the most painful deaths.

HAVE YOU EVER REALIZED THAT IT TAKES MORE ENERGY TO FIGHT FOR YOURSELF THAN IT DOES TO YIELD TO GOD?

Sometimes we have to get sick and tired of the way we've been living in order to crawl back to the altar, to look to our God to move on us once again. We don't get to pick a lot of things in this life, but we do get to pick who and what we will worship.

Personally, worship has become a gift not to be taken for granted, as it has kept me sane over the years. I can't tell you how many nights I had to put worship music on so the enemy would leave me alone. I learned early on that where there is worship, the enemy will not stay. If I'm struggling, if I'm getting ready, if I'm driving, if I'm studying, I turn on worship. If I am going to teach or preach, I always take time to worship. I often fall asleep worshipping, or wake and worship throughout the night. In fact, part of my worship act at night is to pray over myself. The Bible tells us in Job 33:13–18 that the Lord speaks to us during our sleep. When I give my sleep over to the Lord, it is my personal act of worship, recognizing that I need God in the night to help me and to minister to areas that need healing. Keeping our worship hat on is the road to recovery.

WORSHIP IS WHERE HEALING LIVES. IT REMINDS US THAT WITHOUT GOD THERE IS NO HOPE FOR CHANGE, BUT WITH GOD EVERYTHING BECOMES POSSIBLE.

Cultivating and making the daily choice to give God every part of us in worship is where kingdom transformation becomes a reality.

One of the things I love about God is how He generously points us in the right direction. I love this about Jesus. He doesn't hide things from us, but rather for us. He shows us the worship He is after here in John 4; worship where His Spirit is welcomed, where there is an honesty that cannot be faked, and where all are welcomed in unity, this is what He is after. See how Jesus is tying all this together? Remember that when Jesus told us this, it was to the rejected, promiscuous woman – it is her that He entrusts with the insight that a new day is coming. Think about this for a minute – there is a worship coming that will get God's attention. It will be absent of criticism and of people dictating who will be welcomed and who will be rejected. It will not be false – people will be honest and truthful before the Lord, hearts will be focused on Him alone. I love the encouragement of this. It is like Jesus looking at this woman, telling her that life won't always be as it is now, that there will be a time when people's outward appearances, and their struggles, won't be a hindrance. When truth comes, when people know God and who they are, then worship will break out and freedom will be ever so present.

Such is the testimony of the Samaritan woman; we see at

the end of chapter 4 that "many of the Samaritans from that town believed in Him because of the woman's testimony, 'He told me everything I ever did'" (verse 39). And if you fast-forward to Acts chapter 8, you see that Philip the evangelist preaches revival in the same place, and reaps a harvest of souls. You know who laid the foundation? That sinful Samaritan woman, who had been such an outcast, became a great soul-winner for Jesus.

Only God can do this. Only Jesus can take our lives, which are often a mess in different areas, and bring not only restoration, but also redemption. This is why the enemy wants to steal your worship for other things. God always uses the hard places, the scars from our lives, to bring hope, and to remind us of what God has done in us, and what He can also do for others. Imagine the scars on this Samaritan woman. Imagine what she had to push through in order to show herself to those who had rejected her before. That had to take a lot of guts to risk rejection again, and with the same people, yet she did it anyway. The power of her encounter with Jesus was more powerful than the pain she had lived with all those years. The risk she took following that encounter impacted so many. You need to know that people relate to your scars. People need to see examples of those who have made it through difficult and painful times. This Samaritan woman led so many to Christ not because of her perfection, but because of her ability to share her story. Don't hide your story! Don't hide your scars!

SOMETIMES WE NEED TO BE REMINDED THAT PEOPLE CAN RELATE TO OUR SCARS, AND TO THE WAY GOD HAS LOVED US INTO PURPOSE. PEOPLE NEED TO KNOW THERE ARE OTHERS WHO CAN RELATE TO THEIR OWN STRUGGLES, THEIR OWN REJECTIONS, AND THEIR OWN ADDICTIONS.

You may be reading this and realizing that there are areas of your life where your worship has been given to other things instead of God. It could be a relationship, a position, money, or even a place within ministry. One of the mistakes we often make is trying to change everything overnight, and focusing on the need to stop the old behaviors. While this intention is good, it doesn't last. If there is an area of your life that needs redirection, then choose to change the focus. In other words, redirect those places within you and focus them to worship God. I do know this, mostly from personal experience: the areas in your life which are giving you the most hassle are probably the places where you need to redirect your worship back to God.

The more your worship is empowered, the less power and focus go to the behavior or patterns in your life that you want to change.

Remember: if God has your worship, then He has you.

CHAPTER 5

Transformed – a journey not a destination

Do not conform to the pattern of this world, but be transformed…

(Romans 12:2)

Not everything that is faced can be changed,
but nothing can be changed until it is faced.

(Lucille Ball)

The one thing we can count on is change. We are always living in change. Life is always changing. Right now in your life, I would bet that you are either heading into change, in the midst of change, or on your way out of something changing. Change is the one constant in our life we can count on.

CHANGE IS INEVITABLE. CHANGE IS A GIVEN. YET, EVEN THOUGH WE KNOW CHANGE WILL HAPPEN TODAY, WE OFTEN STILL TRY AND AVOID, REJECT, RESIST, EVEN AT TIMES RESENT IT.

But I don't believe all change is negative. In fact, if we look at it through the lens of discipleship, it can become an opportunity for growth. An opportunity to allow ourselves to be stretched and changed, in order to let go of the old in us and say "yes" to enter a new world – a world where the old safety nets and security blankets are slowly taken out of our grip.

On this journey it's good to remind ourselves of the old but true cliché, that nothing great ever comes without intersections of change. So, instead of looking at change as something to avoid, what if we look at it as a chance for something greater? We need to let go of the old security blankets and false illusions, and grasp the truth that we do not have control in the world in order to take hold of today. Even to believe we have control is an illusion. We don't get to pick what happens to us, we only get to choose how we respond and react. What if we stretch ourselves by not just trying to "get through" the change, but embracing it? What about being intentional with change?

I mean, let's be intentional. I am a person who believes in being intentional; if I plan for nothing to happen, I should expect nothing to happen. If you think about it, we are intentional about all sorts of things in life. We always make time to plan for the things we value most; we're intentional about taking time off of work for vacation, we're intentional about where we go to eat, where we hang out, or who we hang out with. We are always being intentional about things that we find important, yet the most important thing is usually last on our list.

I believe that everyone has a deep desire to make changes, to live intentionally, and to change the world around them in a positive way, because God has not created us to just exist; He has created us to make a difference. Yet often we spend our lives in a defensive posture, barely having the time to react, respond, or even avoid what's coming at us. If we're not responding to God or where He is taking us, we often find ourselves reacting to what life throws our way. There is nothing more frustrating than having to spend our days reacting to situation after situation we didn't create.

We all have seasons where we barely stay afloat; thank God those are only seasons, not a lifestyle. In fact, if defensive living becomes a lifestyle, we can easily settle into survival mode. Survival mode steals our ability to be on theoffensive and intentional with our choices. Yet it's surprising just how many people live like this. How frustrating is it to go from one difficult thing to the next, not feeling as if your life is changing at all? No matter the case, all of us have choice within our seasons. Even though change is a given, growth is a choice. So, how do we learn from it? Just going through things won't change us. Time, circumstances, and surviving a difficult season don't bring about maturity. In the West there's almost a sense of entitlement when it comes to hardship, where we believe that if we have to go through difficulties, we should at least get something out of it!

I've heard people say, "Well, I don't get why God doesn't bless me over here. If I have to go through this disease, the least God could do is…" The view that "God should at least do this or that…" has become part of our entitlement culture. It's a sad belief system to think that just because we encounter disease, loss, or financial hardship, we are growing closer to Jesus.

HARDSHIP DOESN'T EQUAL A FREE PASS TO MATURITY OR AN ENTITLED LIFE. THE ONLY THING THAT CHANGES US IS A WILLINGNESS TO ALLOW THE HOLY SPIRIT TO TEACH US THROUGH WHATEVER WE ENCOUNTER. GROWTH IS ALWAYS A CHOICE.

We have to decide: What do I want or need to change? What area in my life am I sick of feeling stuck in? Whether it be a position, a relationship, or a situation, things will not change in us for good if we don't make the intentional choice to yield and allow God's Spirit to work within us.

Things don't change in us, or for us, unless we take personal responsibility for them to change. One of the hardest things for me to watch as a leader is to see people who God has gifted, and entrusted with anointing, be passive with it. Passivity has produced many good leaders who could have been great leaders. Over the years I have seen a passivity and apathy which has hurt the church greatly.

Passivity in the believer, especially in leadership, works against what God wants to do because it creates unsafe environments. I've struggled with it in my own life at times and I've seen it in other areas of leadership, where it has caused people to feel unsettled, unsafe, and sadly uncared for.

Passivity in our walk with Jesus is deadly. We cannot expect to go through life with things happening automatically for us.

THOSE WHO CHANGE THE WORLD AROUND THEM ARE FIRST WILLING TO MAKE THE NEEDED CHANGES WITHIN THEM.

We have to make the daily choice to allow God's Spirit not only to lead us, but to teach us.

Taught by God

The Holy Spirit is the teacher, the paraclete, who walks alongside us – but only if we yield, and allow ourselves to be taught. We have to make ongoing decisions to yield to God's Spirit, for Him to mold us, and make us into all we are meant to be.

CHANGE ISN'T ABOUT OUR IDEA OF PERFECTION, BUT A CHOICE TO SURRENDER THAT WHICH NEEDS PERFECTING. IT DOES NOT COME WITHOUT SOME SORT OF STRUGGLE; THAT'S JUST PART OF IT. BUT IF THE STRUGGLES DON'T LEAD TO SURRENDER, IT WILL CREATE MORE FRUSTRATION.

Surrender, and yielding to Christ, is our only hope for what the apostle Paul is talking about concerning transformation. Transformation is the way of the kingdom, because it's the way of our God, but it is impossible without first yielding to Him.

If you want to know an area of your life that needs some surrendering, then ask yourself: "What are the areas in my life that cause me the most frustration?" The places you feel the most frustration personally, within yourself, are probably the areas that you haven't fully surrendered. It's what I mentioned in the previous chapter, that if you look at the areas in your life that cause you the most frustration, they are usually the areas of your life that need to be redirected in your worship of God. Jesus wants to transform our areas of frustration. Throughout His earthly ministry, everywhere He went He brought transformation. Whether the people wanted it or not, everything Jesus touched got transformed.

The world around us doesn't need to be the world within us. Sometimes I feel we focus way too much on what's not right, or how difficult the world around is. The world will always be the world, and everything that comes with it will surround us. Sin abounds in a sinful world because sinful people live in it. We don't have to take a class on how to sin, it just comes naturally. Paul tells us not to conform to it; just because we're surrounded by sin, that doesn't mean we have to say "yes" to it. There is a better way. There is more than what we see.

"Do not conform," Paul says. The word "not" is strong in the Greek, meaning God forbid; it's a complete denial, simply, categorically, absolutely, and objectively. It is a strong encouragement towards a life change. Sometimes the "do not" in our lives may not be about sin, but about comfort. We like living comfortably. We like to have relationships and structures in our life where we can count on stability and consistency. These are not bad unless we put our faith in them. Sometimes God will allow things in our life just to reveal areas where we need to trust Him more.

We are made of body, soul, and spirit, so we must become alive in each area. Sadly, we walk among the living dead – where people are alive physically, but parts of their soul or spirit are not "alive in Christ" as they were made to be. The apostle Paul writes that when we become believers, we become new creatures, a new creation in Christ.

IT'S NOT JUST ABOUT GETTING RID OF THE PAST, AND THE SINFUL WAYS WE USED TO OPERATE FROM, IT'S ABOUT SETTING THE COURSE OF OUR LIFE IN A NEW DIRECTION.

"Do not conform to the pattern of this world" means that there can be two types of pattern in our minds: the pattern of this world and the pattern of another world – the kingdom of God. The patterns of your life are spilling out of what you are conformed to. Ask yourself, "What patterns do I know need to change?" Then ask yourself, "How am I conforming myself to that pattern?" The word translated "conformed" is the word that we get our English word "scheme" from. It means a conforming that's outward, without necessarily any inner change. The word is also translated "fashioned". Paul is saying, "Do not adopt the fashion of this world, or be forced into its mold."

So, we are being influenced and we are being molded, but we decide what form it will take. The choices we make reveal what we are yielding ourselves to. This is two-part. It's not just about stopping old patterns of behavior. If we redirect our worship and our focus, it will influence how we think. Changed behavior is due to a changed way of thinking.

We need to think not about this world, but about the next. The encouragement is not to sit back and let the world pull us in, to fashion or mold us to be like it, but rather to be intentional about turning our thoughts towards God and allowing Him to form us. Conforming is something you do to yourself. Transforming is something God does to you.

IT TAKES REAL COURAGE TO CHOOSE TRANSFORMATION OVER CONFORMITY, TO CHOOSE A NEW WAY OF LIVING. EVERYTHING THAT'S WORTH IT IN LIFE NOT ONLY INVOLVES CHANGE, IT ALSO INVOLVES COURAGE.

The word "transformation" here means metamorphosis. It literally means to be changed from the inside out. The pain of allowing God into the broken areas of our lives is not always easy. We love quick fixes and it would be much easier if we could just go through a healing prayer line for a one-shot deal. But real transformation is hard work. It is often painful to see parts of us that are ugly, but we have to allow God access to do the needed work within us.

Often we notice a pattern that isn't right, and so we try to make ourselves stop it. We know we're eating the wrong things so we plan a diet. We know we're drinking too much so we put ourselves on a drinking fast. We notice we're losing our temper so we repent, take some deep breaths, and pray that it will be better next time. We operate from a mindset of "I have to change this", instead of a mindset of surrender.

> GOD IS NOT INTERESTED IN US CHANGING OUR LIVES; HE IS MORE INTERESTED IN US INVITING HIM IN TO THE PROCESS OF CHANGE.

He could snap His fingers and make us perfect, but that doesn't seem to be what He's after. He wants the invitation, and for us to acknowledge that we cannot do life without Him. God wants our "yes". He wants us to want Him, which means to take hold of Him and open up our lives, so we have to first let go of the old. Sometimes it's as easy as deciding were sick of how were living!

> TRANSFORMATION DOESN'T TAKE PLACE UNLESS THERE IS DISSATISFACTION WITH OUR CURRENT WAY OF LIVING. WE HAVE TO BE FED UP WITH THE OLD TO ELIMINATE THE OPTIONS OF GOING BACK TO HOW IT WAS.

If we leave any door of our life open to the wrong options, we will walk through it. The moment things get difficult, or things turn out different than we planned, we will take the option to escape. If you want to transform your life, get rid of the destructive options in your mind which you keep open just in case.

PEOPLE CHANGE WHEN THEY ARE SO SICK OF THE OLD WAYS THAT, NO MATTER HOW HARD IT IS, GOING BACK IS NOT AN OPTION.

If we are half-hearted, we will only offer parts of ourselves to God. True transformation isn't about only surrendering the parts to God we feel comfortable with, but rather inviting Him in to every part of who we are. Inviting the Holy Spirit into our lives is choosing to give up control. The Holy Spirit is referred to as the wind or a dove in the Scriptures: how can you pocket the wind or tell a bird how to fly? To invite God's Spirit is to relinquish control, which means choosing vulnerability as we present ourselves back to God. We are to present ourselves as "living sacrifices" with the understanding that there is no such thing as partial sacrifice or a partial commitment. It is impossible to be "sort of committed". There's a difference between a decision and a commitment. We can decide to show up to church and show our gratitude by worshipping God, which of course is so important, but true commitment lasts, no matter the difficulty.

Being fully committed means we allow God access to every part of us, even the parts we're ashamed or embarrassed of.

Instead of using our bodies for what we want – or think we want – we should instead present them as a gift back to God. This is a holy act, which pleases Him. It's a very spiritual decision to give yourself to God and allow Him to do His best work within you.

> Take, Lord, and receive all my liberty,
> my memory, my understanding
> and my entire will,
> All I have and call my own.
>
> You have given all to me.
> To you, Lord, I return it.
>
> Everything is yours; do with it what you will.
> Give me only your love and your grace.
> That is enough for me.
>
> St. Ignatius of Loyola

I love the NLT version of Romans 12:2 which says, "Don't copy the behavior and customs of this world, but let God transform you into a new person by changing the way you think." It is impossible to have lasting change without the provision of God's power – without yielding and surrendering to the One who holds the power to transform us. The key is to let God; it is not something we can do ourselves. For years I have thought, "If I could just get stronger; if I could just stop this behavior, or change that attitude, or get myself motivated to change..." But you know what I found? I found more frustration. I wanted to give up, and I wanted to quit even trying. There were times it may have worked for a little while, or I would see some progress and get excited. But the minute I went backwards, I felt worse than when I had started.

TRANSFORMING AREAS OF OUR LIFE IS NOT ABOUT GETTING A STRONGER WILL,
BUT RATHER A SURRENDERED WILL.

Transformation is always about surrender. The more surrendered we are to the Holy Spirit, the freer we become.

The transforming power of love

As a mom, of course I want my kids to live out what they've been made for, but also I want them to go above and beyond my wildest dreams for them. Why? Because I love them deeply, and it's my love for them which causes me to pray that they would make decisions that take them into what they were created for. Love always desires the best.

It is the deep love of God towards you that sees your potential, and desires that it would come to pass. One of the most amazing things about the sovereignty of God is that He doesn't just see us as we are; He sees what we are made to be. If you read through the Gospels and see how Jesus ministered to people, His invitations were always to enter into more; His words, especially to those with great needs, seemed to be encouragements to rise above their current situations and struggles, and see that they were better than they realized.

The invitation to transformation is founded on God's love for you. God is not interested in you managing your sin; the goal is not to work your way into perfection, but rather to lean into Him, trusting His love for you. Even where we lack perfection, we are loveable. From the place of love comes the invitation to trust the

One who loves us best. You will not surrender to God if you don't trust Him. Ask yourself if there is any area of your life where you are worried about Him coming through. Some of you had very hurtful relationships with your earthly father, so to trust God without the fear of being let down or rejected is something you have had to work through. Even lousy relationships with others can affect how we see, and trust, God.

If we aren't trusting God in an area of our life, we have to ask why. An inability to surrender stunts our growth. Only when we know God will come through will we then trust Him with our life. It is in the freedom of surrendering to God that His power enables us to let go of the old and take on the new. This is where new life in us begins to take shape. This is also why the enemy will make it difficult to yield. He knows if you trust and yield yourself to God, then you become a threat. Some of my greatest nights of lost sleep have been times when I fought surrender. Whether it was the enemy harassing me or me harassing myself, surrender is not always an easy road.

We only become alive in Christ when we are surrendered to Christ. Being alive in Christ means we will be full of action, awakened to a new purpose and a realization of what we were created for. If you look at people who are doing what they know they are meant to be doing with their lives, not only does it bring a great satisfaction, but it also changes their appearance – literally! People shine when they are alive in Christ, because to live and operate in purpose is to reflect the One who made us. When an artist creates a masterpiece, it is only when the work is brought into the light for others to see that it gives insight into the artist. One reflects the other.

If we are not shining, then we are not alive in quite the way we are called to be alive. People are dead in so many ways. There is a great quote I saw years ago that said, "Many walk around with saved souls but lost lives." Every part of you is meant to shine, every part of you, body, soul, and spirit, to come to life. Usually we focus on the body, however if you shut down parts of your soul or spirit, you often remain unaware that they are shut down, until they are awakened in some way.

For some of you reading this, my story is your story; there are areas in your life where you have yet to come to life. Perhaps others of you have boxed God – or know there are places within yourself that are hidden – but you don't know another way. Perhaps some of you live in the sadness of having areas in your life where you have lost hope for change. Others of you may have a nicely ordered life, and be productive in it. God may even be using you in incredible ways, yet you have pockets of frustration which you have put off to the side, because you don't expect them ever to change.

Whether some of these things, all of these things, or none of these things apply to you, I encourage you to ask God. Personally, I have never once gone before God and received the answer that all is good! As long as we're alive, there is change that needs to happen in each of us.

GOD'S DESIRE IS NOT THAT WE WOULD SPEND OUR LIFE TRYING TO AVOID THE WORLD; RATHER HIS DESIRE IS THAT WE WOULD TRUST HIM ENOUGH TO SURRENDER OUR WORLD TO HIM.

If you are willing to ask Him what needs to be changed, He will reveal these areas to you.

TO HAVE AREAS OF OUR LIFE THAT NEED TO BE TRANSFORMED DOESN'T MEAN WE ARE ANY LESS POWERFUL, OR LESS SPIRITUAL, IT JUST MEANS WE ARE HUMAN.

Some of the most godly, productive people I know have deep areas of brokenness which God continues to work on. Everyone has areas of weakness, it is just a matter of whether or not they are willing to admit it.

There have been many times where I have felt the terror of feeling stuck, guilty, or overwhelmed, sometimes feeling all of them at once, but we are not left alone without hope. In fact, if you are reading this, it is probably God's moment for you. If you feel trapped, there is always hope for change. If you feel hopeless, you may actually be in just the right place for God to work. You are not crazy; you are human. As humans, we all have broken areas in our lives that only the One who created us can heal.

Only God can cause life to exist, and only God can cause us to shine in the way we were called to shine. It is never a one-shot deal, and is never fully realized this side of heaven, but what I have learned, and am still learning, is that God always wants us to work towards transformation. **The kingdom of God isn't about changing areas of our life so we feel better about ourselves; the kingdom of God is about transforming areas of our life so we can reflect more of who our Creator is.** This is all part of the journey. The transformation process is to heal our way into wholeness. We have to remind ourselves the destination isn't the point, but rather the loving and healing power of Jesus as we continue to trust Him more and more.

1 Peter 2:24 tells us that by His wounds we have been healed. The word used for "healing" here is the same word we find for wholeness. God's desire is that we will be whole – the entire person: body, soul, and spirit. The transforming power of God is His healing power. He begins to heal and make right areas in us that need restoring. Too often the church, especially in the more charismatic circles, heavily focuses on the physical aspect of healing, yet there is so much more.

There is always more for us; no one is superhuman or perfect, or has everything figured out. Now some of you may be in church leadership and maybe don't believe that there are parts of you that are broken, or that you need a deeper encounter of trusting God. You may have a successful ministry or life, and God may even be blessing everything you put your hand to. Success, gifts, anointing, and even power, don't mean that we don't have areas where God wants to change us. We mustn't misunderstand the presence and power of God, and how He uses us, to mean that we don't also need time for healing and change and restoration. Healing is ongoing, because the battle is ongoing. Just because God uses me doesn't mean I'm not broken in some areas.

The gospel means good news. Isaiah chapter 61 is the picture of why Jesus came; it illustrates why the King of Glory chose to invade our world. The Father saw the condition of our world and chose to save, to rescue, to redeem and restore, each and every person. This is the gospel, the gospel to the poor – which is all of us.

> The Lord has anointed me to proclaim good news to the poor. He has sent me to bind up the brokenhearted, to proclaim freedom for the captives and release from darkness for the prisoners.

(Isaiah 61:1–2)

But if we just take this part of the King's message, it refers not just to the physical, but also to our spiritual and emotional condition. Oppression is depression. It is found all through Isaiah, in Luke 4, and all through the Gospels, and it means the inability to move. So many people aren't shining in their purpose, or feel the weight of not changing, that they can't even get out of bed in the morning.

Oppression is the picture of the enemy in action. It causes people to feel hopeless, under a heavy weight of pressure. Where we find oppression, we find the enemy at work. However, every time we see where God's people are oppressed, we find the promise that He Himself will rise up and defend them. This is God's heart towards those who feel that life will never change, and where the heaviness of what's wrong overrides even the good things of life. Here we find Christ, who came to defend, restore, and redeem. If you struggle with these feelings and hardships, you need to know that God Himself rises up to defend you. He is there and He is near, even if you don't feel Him; His promise to you is that He will never leave nor forsake you. Sometimes the hardest time to trust this truth is when we don't feel it.

It is during these times that we need to remind ourselves to rest on the promises of God.

THE SCRIPTURES ARE THE VERY WORDS OF GOD WHICH REMIND US OF THE TRUTHS ABOUT GOD. TRUTH IS NOT SOMETHING GOD GIVES, TRUTH IS WHO GOD IS.

The truth is that God is with you. One of the names of God is **El Roi** – the God who sees me. I love this. I love that the God who created me also sees me – even my struggles, and the areas I am embarrassed by. There is so much hope in this, because the God who sees is also the God who restores. God hasn't just saved our soul but continues to restore us along the way. He is also **Rapha**, meaning our healer. God is our physician, He is the One to heal our hurts, even the distress we carry in this life. His healing goes way beyond the physical, as it touches every part of who we are. To heal us physically is to heal us spiritually and emotionally as well. How can we not be moved when we know God reaches into our lives and cares about our pain, no matter the condition? Even when we read through the Gospels, how people got sick was never the point. **When Jesus was ministering, He seemed to be more concerned about the person hurting than how they had got into the dilemma they were in.** How people got sick was never the point in Jesus' ministry. **Sometimes we don't allow God into areas that need transformation because we're so ashamed of how we got sick. Don't allow the shame of what needs healing to be bigger than God's desire to see you, but also heal you.** I am not discounting sin, or the importance of caring for our bodies, but we need to know how God sees us, and His deep desire to move on us in ways He knows we are in need of. He is fully aware that each of us carries pain in different ways and He not only sympathizes, He is moved with compassion on our behalf. This in itself brings healing. It brings healing in the way of peace to my mind knowing I am not left alone, but I have One that cares about how I feel and what I may be having to endure. Transformation involves every part of who we are. He is the One who "forgives all your sins and heals all your diseases" (Psalm 103:3).

To be forgiven is to be healed. To be released from the guilt of sin brings healing in a deep way that we can't explain, or live without once we have experienced it. But to be healed of our diseases as well is another level. We have tended to address disease as being a physical condition, such as cancer, diabetes, or various physical ailments. However, the word "disease" does not mean just physical problems, it means suffering. To suffer is to hurt in our soul. Suffering affects not only the body, it affects our emotions and feelings, often even our will, and the ability to get up and choose to want change. Only Jesus can heal these parts of us that need healing.

God's promise is to bring healing in our suffering; this is another reminder that we are never alone, and it is often in the hardest times that we need to be reminded the most that God is ever so present. Our physical bodies may not be completely healed, but there is always a deep work of healing if God is with us. Where God is, is where healing is. We cannot box God and say that just because the physical suffering is still present, God is ignoring us or doing nothing. As long as God is present some form of healing is taking place: "He heals the brokenhearted and bandages their wounds" (Psalm 147:3 NLT). This means our wounds, pain, hurt, injury, even sorrow. It again points to the physical, but is also emotional.

It doesn't make any sense for someone to say that they are fully healed, or fully restored. This is a picture of the ongoing invitation of God's desire for us to allow Him into the places of our wounds, sorrows, pain, and suffering. As long as we are on this earth we are in a battle which produces wounds; to some extent, everyone is hurt or injured in some way. These battle wounds don't only affect those who know God; saved or unsaved, no one comes out of battle unscathed. Living on the front lines produces wounds that only the Healer can heal.

As the church, it's vital we don't just focus on the physical health of a person. In fact, we can't expect others around us to change, let alone change ourselves, unless we're offering an opportunity for people to be honest about their condition.

WE DON'T GET TO PICK WHAT PEOPLE BECOME ADDICTED TO, OR HOW THEY BECOME WORN OUT, TROUBLED, OR DISCOURAGED. BUT IT'S VITAL IN ORDER FOR REAL CHANGE TO HAPPEN WITHIN THE CHURCH THAT WE MINISTER AND GIVE SPACE FOR HEALING AND ACCEPTANCE OF THE WHOLE PERSON.

Many times we're praying for a leg to be healed, when in fact the heart is hurting. So many times I am looking for people to change, not realizing that there are deeper issues to their pain. But the message to the church, and through the church, is that we are to live in transformation, so we must address the whole person in order for true transformation to take place in the world around us.

Too many are suffering in silence because they aren't changing, yet the pressure to change is great. There is nothing harder than knowing something needs to change but feeling powerless to do anything about it. We have to ask ourselves if we are really allowing space for people to change. So many Christians continue to say "yes" to the world, conforming to what's easier rather than allowing themselves to surrender to the God they have been presented with.

WE SHOULD NOT BE SURPRISED AT THE WAYS IN WHICH PEOPLE ARE CONFORMING, BUT RATHER ALLOW SPACE – FOR OURSELVES AND OTHERS – TO REALIZE THAT THE GOD WHO SEES, SEES US.

Are we allowing people to be seen – do we really see their suffering?

Transforming lives

The areas in you that need to be transformed are the areas Jesus came to restore. Often the very parts of us we hide from God are the very parts that He wants to transform. Healing is change and change is healing, but until we realize that God desires to transform every part of us, we will stick to the old ways of ministering, to ourselves and others, and therefore we won't see the deeper transformation take place in us, or in the lives of the people around us. Transformation is not a destination, but a journey. If we aren't willing to journey with people, then we've discounted much of how God works in bringing people into wholeness. Transformation is a process, not an overnight miracle.

We all need this truth for ourselves, but also for the world. Our life is never just about us. God is so economical that when He is at work in you, it is always for the benefit of the people around you too.

We all need to be transformed, our countries need transformation; in fact it's obvious to the world that there is much change needed. Yet needing change is not a popular thing to talk about in church. It's not popular to focus on what's wrong; it's not even a popular message in the church to talk about where or what is broken. But we cannot change what we do not first acknowledge. The world around us is hurting in ways that we, as the church, have not acknowledged.

I am so amazed at the goodness of God's transforming power, which I have seen at work over many years in the church. I have watched countless people come to know Jesus. I have seen miracles in ways I never dreamed possible. And I feel incredibly privileged to have trained people to see these things for themselves. I have watched so many receive physical healing from Jesus. I have seen people learn to pray for others for the first time. It is the goodness of God watching Him love on people in so many different ways. But I have also seen the church get stuck. We tend to see where God moved, or how He worked, or healed, and we tend to take that incident and build from it, expecting for it to stay that way forever.

Remember, the church operated for centuries without the Spirit of God. It is very easy for any leader, church, or ministry to live and operate from what they know. Let's face it, the church loves to take what God's done, put their stamp on it, and sell it. **We often get stuck in models and formulas, and God is not a formula to be used, but a relationship to be lived out.** In fact if you spend your time trying to figure out the formula of God, you will find yourself extremely frustrated. Healing comes from relationship, and wholeness comes because we've encountered Rapha, our great healer. It's a by-product of intimacy in relationship as there is no way that we can be loved by God and not be changed by God.

The trouble is, it seems that we find something that works, and we camp there. Sometimes we even try to manipulate God to make our life, church, or gatherings more exciting. But I find this to be a very slippery slope; some start to believe that we can even use the gift of faith to see what we can get God to do. But sometimes it's a sober and needed reminder to us that God is not on display for our entertainment.

We have to see, hear, and know what our very personal God is doing today, because what God has done in us, or in the church throughout the years, may not be what's effective now. When I think of those who travelled throughout their country to share the gospel, many on foot or on horseback, I can't help but be incredibly grateful that I was not born in that generation! I don't think I would have lasted! The world is changing, life is evolving, and if we don't tune in to what's happening in the world around us today, we cannot serve effectively. In order to work with God, we must be willing to open our eyes and look, tune our ears to hear, and ask ourselves, "What are people hurting with? Where are the broken? Where are the poor? Where are those who are mourning or without hope?" We do not have to look far.

I believe it's vital that the church sees, hears, and is attentive to how God desires to heal the world around us today. I love what God has done in the area of physical healing in the last thirty years, but many of the hurts and pains of today are louder in other ways. All around us today people are suffering with mental illness in ways we have never seen before. Whether it is within the church or not, there is probably not one family that isn't struggling themselves or caring for someone with a mental illness. The statistics are staggering. One in four Brits and one in five Americans either struggle with, or care for those with, a mental illness.

I cannot tell you the number of people I have prayed for in the last several years alone who are godly people, but are living with depression or anxiety, or caring for someone who is bipolar or has learning disabilities. I feel such deep sadness when I hear how the church has responded to their struggles, with comments such as, "Are you praying enough?" "Anxiety is from the devil, so where are you empowering the devil?" "Why are you still sick? We've prayed for you many times already. Are you sure you want help? Are you sure you want to get well?"

Suffering, especially those who suffer with chronic illnesses, is not a popular topic within charismatic circles. Often we don't mind you having the condition, but if you're still suffering after we have prayed for you, then where is your faith lacking? We have confused suffering, or struggling, with a lack of faith. We don't like to acknowledge that suffering is actually in the New Testament, and if our Savior endured suffering, why would we be above Him? **Suffering is scary because often we don't have any clear-cut answers… It also doesn't fit into the "heaven now" belief culture that has worked its way into the church.**

We have approached ministry for those struggling with mental health issues, for themselves or others, with a healing prayer-line model. We prayed, but if it's not changing for you, then your faith must be lacking. Therefore, sadly much of the church has a reputation for doing more harm than good in these situations. We have approached people's struggles as if we can fix them. I have prayed for so many people who are on depression medication, or other various types of medicines that are to do with their brain chemistry, yet they feel as if something is wrong with them for even asking for help. The stigma attached to taking medication for mental illness almost takes us back to the dark ages.

It makes no sense. If you had to take medicine for cancer, hopefully you would get sympathy, empathy, and all kinds of prayer and support from the local church. But mental illness is not popular; with mental illness we find shame and stigma.

It feels like one of the unreachable problems of our day. Usually if we think that something is unreachable or unchangeable within us, then we resign ourselves to the belief that it is just how our life is, so we will have to learn to live with it. In the church, things that we feel are too difficult to address or handle often get left to the government, but wherever you live, a government cannot bring healing to your soul. It cannot do what God has created His church to do. And we as the church must not ignore things in us or in the world around us that need change just because of the fear or difficulty attached to them.

It is not popular to hang around with those who are sick these days. Pray for them yes, but to hang out, or invite the suffering into our world, especially if they carry stigma because of their struggles? We would rather they went somewhere else. I truly believe that in order for the church to minister effectively in the coming years, we must engage with, and truly see, the culture around us. We must recognize that the sick, the wounded, and the suffering are struggling with painful conditions of the mind, body, and soul that the church has yet to recognize. A great encouragement to all of us is that **Jesus didn't hang out with who, or what, was popular; in fact, where we find the stigma is where we find our Jesus.**

If the souls of those in the culture around us are hurting deeply, but they are afraid of coming clean, then this is where the enemy has a field day; he always does his best work in silence and isolation. **True transformation, in us and the world around, will only take place where there is safety in honesty** – where people know that if they admit their struggles, they won't be judged or rejected.

Nobody wants to be rejected. No one wants to be left out. The great and wonderful truth about the gospel is that it is all-inclusive. The invitation of God's transforming, healing power is for all who are willing to say "yes". This means that we must adjust to allow space for God to move in us and others.

WE ARE, AT BEST, WORKS IN PROGRESS.

The start of God transforming His church is the church realizing that we all need transformation, but also keeping the person – not the struggle – as the focus.

Paul said it best in 2 Corinthians 4:7–16:

> But we have this treasure in jars of clay to show that this all-surpassing power is from God and not from us. We are hard pressed on every side, but not crushed; perplexed, but not in despair; persecuted, but not abandoned; struck down, but not destroyed. We always carry around in our body the death of Jesus, so that the life of Jesus may also be revealed in our body. For we who are alive are always being given over to death for Jesus' sake, so that his life may also be revealed in our mortal body. So then, death is at work in us, but life is at work in you. It is written: "I believed; therefore I have spoken." Since we have that same spirit of faith, we also believe and therefore speak, because we know that the one who raised the Lord Jesus from the dead will also raise us with Jesus and present us with you to himself. All this is for your benefit, so that the grace that is reaching more and more people may cause thanksgiving to overflow to the glory of God. Therefore we do not lose heart. Though

outwardly we are wasting away, yet inwardly we are being renewed day by day.

Paul reminds us that although we are all chosen to be used by God, we are all broken in various ways. Not one person, no matter where they come from, or even how much God is using them, is above being broken or having some area of weakness. We all have areas that need continual work. Knowing this, yet not having the space and freedom to come clean, not only frustrates people, but also allows no room for true freedom or true transformation to take place. Fear of rejection has kept many from being honest about their struggles. But transformation is needed for everyone because the gospel is for everyone. Transformation must infiltrate every area of the church, including its leaders.

When we view people as superhuman, or anointed, or untouchable, we don't leave any space for them to be human. Just because someone is on the stage doesn't mean they have everything together. There seems to be a misunderstanding that church titles or positions create perfect people. I am always on the stage and my life is far from perfect. When we set people up as perfect, we set them up for failure. The Internet, stadium events, and stage ministries have given a false illusion of perfection. I have prayed for too many people who are hiding their struggles because people around them have put them on a pedestal.

We mustn't confuse God's perfection, His ministry, and His gifts, with God using us, and think that it is our greatness. Just because someone preaches from the stage one night doesn't mean they're doing altar calls at the breakfast table at their home the next morning. Never once have I got up in the morning to my kids giving me a standing ovation! Don't get me wrong, when it comes to character, yes, it should be the same on and off the stage. And truth is, many of those things happening on the stage do happen on a smaller scale at the dinner table, or over coffee, or taking walks with people. But when God is using someone in their gifting, that is called anointing. And people often see anointing as powerful, courageous, untouchable, thick-skinned – often mistaking the anointing for how the person lives day in and day out, whereas actually, God anoints us for certain tasks.

Anointing is what happens when God favors us to do things which we could not do apart from Him. But this doesn't mean, just because someone is anointed for teaching or ministry, that they are somehow different. We live in a culture where many find it hard to separate the stage life from the life of the person. We are all just humans serving our God with the gifts He chooses to give to us. In fact, this might shock some of you, but even pastors are human!

It is so sad, but I have watched many of my friends move powerfully as God used them in front of thousands, only to hear the critics come and tear them apart, thinking they are doing God a favor. "This person is so strong and powerful, what I say won't hurt them." As if they think that they aren't even human. Don't mistake the anointing of God with someone being superhuman. It's not true and it's not godly. It also works against the purposes of God.

The greatest call of the church is to bring all people into the transformational power of the gospel.

BUT IF WE EXCLUDE PEOPLE BASED ON WHO WE THINK SHOULD BE ALLOWED THE SPACE TO CHANGE, WE TAKE AWAY THE ROOM FOR HONESTY AND HEALING.

It hurts the church and it's a quick path to disappointment. You don't even have to be a church leader for someone to have had unrealistic expectations of you that discouraged or overwhelmed you – we either get disappointed, or we are the disappointment! One of my dreams is to see the church become the safest place where people, including leaders, can open up and be free to work towards real change, and get well without the fear of judgment.

If the church doesn't create space for freedom, who will?

It doesn't really matter what you do, where you live, or how many people know about it. What matters is you need space for freedom in your own life, and so do the people around you. We need to remind each other that it is what we do and who we are that matters. Wherever you serve, you are just as important as the one who serves alongside of you. As Henry Adams once said, "He too serves a certain purpose who only stands and cheers." Every part matters. No one part is more important than another. Your stage may be different than mine, but to God they are both of equal value.

Everyone's stage is different. But if God has placed you to serve "behind the scenes", then go for it. It is just as important to God as the person who is visible. Every act of service matters, and one is just as important as another. Run with people who encourage you to grow, and give you space to grow. I believe that our relationships, and who we run with, are so important. No matter what you do in life, you have to have people around you that build you up and who always encourage you to go after more of Jesus.

The community you have around you either makes you or breaks you. The enemy is quick to use people who, because of their own insecurity, will do or say things to undermine how God will use you. Don't wait for it, but don't be surprised by it either. No matter the stage of influence God has given you, whether it is large or small, you still have to remember that you're human, and your willingness to admit your weaknesses opens the door for you to encounter more of Jesus.

Allow yourself space, and be intentional about making choices towards real change. A transformed life isn't a destination, it is saying "yes" to the journey.

Start with yourself; allow yourself to change by admitting to the broken places and areas of weakness where you need the intervention of God. Remember, if growth is a by-product of change, then there will always be great resistance to it – whether it comes from ourselves or those around us, we can count on a struggle! The enemy doesn't just stand aside when you decide to change. He doesn't let go easily, and sometimes there are things that we have lived with for years, which will not necessarily be easily changed overnight.

THE VERY PLACE THAT GOD IS DOING HIS DEEPEST WORK IN YOU IS WHERE YOU WILL FIND THE ENEMY HARASSING YOU THE MOST. JUST REMEMBER, THE ENEMY ALWAYS GETS THE LOUDEST RIGHT BEFORE HE IS ABOUT TO GET SHUT DOWN.

Don't listen to his accusations, but focus your worship on God who is the only One who has the power to transform you.

There have been times in my own life where I have had to push through what feels like insurmountable opposition. Don't be surprised if you want to quit, give up, or run away. Be kind to yourself, and remember to eliminate the options of running or quitting. Don't leave those other options open in your mind, because the options that you keep in the back of your mind will become a front door when things get tough. Never leave unhealthy options open. Put them out of your mind. Options and negotiations cannot have a place in surrendering our lives to God.

Also, don't be surprised if the enemy tries to make you fear that change is not possible. Hold on to the truth, meditate on what God says, and allow His voice to win out over every other voice. Every time I feel fearful, I know at the core of me that it is the enemy trying to shut down that which has the potential to change not only me, but those around me. God always has more for us, and with any change that has deep potential, the enemy will do what he can to stop it. Ask yourself: who has the most to gain from me having less of God? It is possible to get to the place where the fear that is intended to shut us down can be used to fuel our fire, when we determine that we will not allow the enemy to have his way in that area of our life any longer.

If God invites us into transformation, that means it is His idea, and whatever God says is what we can count on to be true, no matter the fear, the struggle, the pain, the wound, or the suffering. Surrender to Jesus, and Jesus will in turn not only give you what you need, He will take you farther than you ever dreamed possible.

CHAPTER 6

Project Renovation: renewing the mind

Do not conform [...] but be transformed by the renewing of your mind.

(Romans 12:2)

How you think is how you live: the power of a person's life being transformed is the result of an ongoing decision to yield. The more we yield to the Spirit of God, allowing Him to align our thought life, the freer and more productive we become.

In 2 Corinthians 5:17, we find Paul's dramatic declaration that we have become a new creation in Christ: the new creation of our "spirit man". The real you is your spirit man, which was made alive in Christ when you first said "yes" to His call. God has placed eternity in the heart of each man and woman. There is no such thing as a bad creation in God's eyes; there is only one

Creation, and all of us are made in His image, in the likeness of our Creator. God's desire is that "none should perish" (2 Peter 3:9), but many choose to perish none the less. **All of life comes down to choices, and even though God has planted eternity in you, you have to decide whom you will spend eternity with.** From the moment we are born, until the moment we die, we are preparing for eternity. It's a wonder we put so much emphasis and importance on the material things of this life when they're such a tiny part of our existence.

Our existence is found only in Christ, and from this starting place until we are with Him for eternity, we are getting ourselves ready for the next life, as it is our character that we take with us. We are three parts – spirit, soul, and body; man is a spirit; he has a soul; and he lives in a body. Just as we train our body and soul, we must continue to be trained in our spirit. We were created with a spirit so that we could relate to God who is Spirit. "Those who are led by the Spirit of God are the children of God" (Romans 8:14). It's our spirit which cries, "Abba, Father," meaning papa. Through our spirit we communicate with God directly. That's why chapter 8 of Romans deals with the Spirit-led life, and with building our spirit man, because that is how we relate so personally with our God.

The enemy will fight against you building up your spirit man, because if this gets strong, then it feeds your trust and transformation journey with God. One of the strongest ways the enemy will try to keep you at a distance is by using condemnation. Condemnation is one of the things that must be addressed on our journey of strengthening our spirit man.

Paul has to address condemnation before he addresses how we communicate with God, because it is condemnation which causes us to shrink back from fully engaging in close connection with God the Father, our "Papa". Condemnation is one of those words we can feel the weight of when we hear it. The dictionary definition of condemnation is to express disapproval of; to pronounce sentence against; or to declare unfit for use. We feel the weight of those things we've done wrong. We wouldn't be human if we didn't have a conscience. But over us Christ says that "there is now no condemnation" (Romans 8:1), which means there is no disapproval in how God sees us. We are now fit to be used. The word "now" here is so important because it is the "now" that matters, not the past. The past is no longer to dictate how we go forward.

Having no condemnation and no disapproval from our God means that we have been freed from judgment – Jesus took that out of our hands. You don't even have the right to judge yourself. Paul doesn't say, "there is no accusation against them", because there is. The enemy doesn't always use lies against you to deter you; he often uses things about your life which are true. Notice that Paul doesn't say, "there is nothing in them that deserves condemnation", because we have all sinned and done wrong. But if we belong to the Lord, then being "in Him" means that the case against us is thrown out.

HAVE YOU EVER NOTICED THAT IN THE SCRIPTURES GOD SPEAKS MORE ABOUT WHAT WE HAVE IN HIM THAN WHAT WE HAVE DONE WRONG?

Hans Selye, who was known for his studies on the human body and the effects of stress, said this: "As much as we thirst for approval, we dread condemnation." In all of us there is a deep-seated angst that we should be justly condemned for our wrongdoing. In fact, the basis of all religion is to be aware that we are indeed broken, and need to somehow pay for our choices. All through the centuries we hear of different ways people offered self-inflicted punishment for their own personal brokenness, including flagellation, which means a flogging, whipping, or lashing out. It is the act of methodically beating the human body with special implements, such as whips, lashes, or rods, to punish and condemn people and their behavior. Some countries still have these practices today. Many people feel that they should "pay a price" for their wrongs, and the idea that God would come and wash them clean, without some form of punishment, is a difficult concept for many.

The practice of abusing one's self (self-flagellation), as penance for atonement of sins and a path to sanctity, is a mortification of the flesh. This seems to be fairly common these days, because so many people live self-destructively, feeling as if they don't deserve much of a life. So many young people self-harm by cutting themselves, believing they need to pay for their lack of self-worth. The devil is a tormentor, stealing the truth that when God sees you, He approves of you. You are not a disappointment. To understand the power of the words "there is now no condemnation in Christ Jesus" is to step into the journey of transformation.

YIELDING TO THE TRANSFORMING POWER OF GOD IS AN INVITATION TO AN ONGOING LIFESTYLE; IT IS NOT A DESTINATION TO REACH, BUT A SAYING "YES" TO THE JOURNEY.

If God has said the past has gone, then that means your past has gone! You may have some residue of consequence from your past, but going forward, the focus must not be on what is wrong with you, but on the truth of what Christ has done, and has said over your life.

John 3:16 says: "For God so loved the world that He gave…" But then verse 17 says: "For God did not send His Son into the world to condemn the world, but to save the world through Him." We often confuse the conviction of God with condemnation. How do we know the difference between condemnation and the conviction of the Holy Spirit? Condemnation will accuse you, and take you into bondage, but God's Spirit convicts in order to lead you into freedom. Conviction from Christ is always for our betterment. Conviction comes from the Holy Spirit, but condemnation comes from judgment. God's Spirit within us not only guides, comforts, and walks alongside us, but the Holy Spirit also convicts. When God's Spirit is convicting us, He is revealing an area in our life where we are settling for less than what He has created us for.

The Bible states that there is now "no condemnation in Christ", meaning that it is only outside of Christ where condemnation abounds. This also reveals the inclusion of the gospel – it is for all people, everyone is invited, each and every person has the right to say "yes". But it also mentions the exclusion – not all will say "yes" to Jesus. The promise is only for those who are "in Christ", where freedom from condemnation is found.

Therefore, anytime we take ourselves outside of Christ is when the enemy has freedom to torment us with condemnation. The freedom to live in Christ always begins and ends with our minds, for whatever we think is then how we live. How is your thought life? How do you see yourself? How do you see your family, your business, and your working relationships? How do you see God? Your answers are a reflection of what's going on in your thought life. Sometimes we do not realize that our thinking has taken us outside of God's best.

Have you been in a period of life where you felt that generally things were pretty good? The family is doing well, you're somewhat pleased with your job, your work relationships are going smoothly, and God may even be using you in great ways. Things for the most part are going well.

And then life happens.

Something you weren't planning comes in sideways and it feels as if your time of tranquility is over. It may be something which completely disrupts your life, or it could just be a rather unpleasant exchange with someone which has left you feeling rattled. I have found that these moments, these exchanges in life, are when God is at work. Somehow, in some way, God is intervening in your life, and what He is allowing to be a disruption isn't as important as how you respond to it.

IT SEEMS THAT GOD IS MORE CONCERNED WITH WHETHER WE WILL YIELD AND TRUST HIM, THAN WITH US ARRIVING AT A COMFORTABLE DESTINATION.

Every invitation to change is a moment in which God, in some way, gets our attention. It's different for all of us. How God gets your attention will be different to how He reaches me. One thing I do know is that the longer we walk with God, the more these moments happen – moments in our lives where the way we are currently living gets a bit disrupted, and we realize that something in us needs to change. These **God moments usually reveal themselves in times we didn't expect, from people or places we would never have thought of, and rarely do we find them the most comfortable places.** I have had hundreds, if not thousands, of these moments in my relationship with God, where He has intervened to get my attention.

I had one of these God interventions a few years ago.

I was sitting with a friend, chatting about what was happening in my life, and as we were talking my friend gently said, "You know, Christy, you say, 'I don't really like doing that' a lot."

First, I thought it was a joke. It was not.

I quickly realized my friend was serious, which took me off guard, because much of what we were talking about involved some of the ministry I was doing. I have done so many sermons, interviews, and conversations, and I had always felt that I loved, or at least liked, what I was doing. This was the first time that I'd had feedback about the ministry I was doing that took me off guard. One reason I was surprised was because she was so honest with me, having no concern for how risky that could have been. And secondly, my friend's boldness and frankness – without judgment – disarmed me to the place where it freed my mind to be really honest.

As we talked, I felt like I was acknowledging something which up until that point had been untouchable. I realized there was something I had believed about ministry – that even if I didn't like parts of what I was doing, the actual words "I don't like it" seemed really wrong to think, let alone say. But that's what being disarmed with love and kindness can do. When your armor is off you can see and feel things that you couldn't before.

IT'S GOOD TO WEAR SOME ARMOR TO PROTECT YOURSELF, BUT NOT SO THAT
GOD CAN'T HAVE ACCESS TO RESTORE YOUR SOUL.

These God moments are usually times where God is asking us to take our armor off.

This moment brought me the realization that I had areas of my mind and heart where I had protected myself in an unhealthy way. The spiritual protection God gives us is vital, but the personal walls we put up to try to protect ourselves from life can hurt us deeply. I began to see that where my self-protection may have kept me from harm, it had also protected me from more of Jesus. When my guard was down, I allowed myself to not only see, but to recognize a few areas where I had been shut down, and the more I opened up the more I began to spill.

The truth was that not only did I not like some of what I was doing, I felt guilty for feeling that way. I felt guilty to even think about change in this area of my life. I felt tremendous condemnation towards myself, not because of sin, but because I had some false belief systems about myself in serving the Lord. If you feel condemned, it doesn't necessarily mean that you are in sin – the enemy loves to keep us trapped in condemnation for any reason.

When I began chatting with my friend, my heart was exposed. With the heart exposed things in us begin to spill out, often not what we think, or what we want, but what is actually happening inside of us. Who we are deep inside is the place that we spill from. This reveals the power of our thought life. I never would have believed that I would think these things about myself, or the ministry, or my walk with God, yet it was clear the enemy had hold of my mind in a few areas. **The mind is so powerful that it has our hearts and mouths attached to it.** Our parts are so interconnected that every thought, everywhere our mind dwells, really matters. What we end up talking about doesn't spill out of nowhere; whether it is good, bad, or ugly, what comes out of our mouths just shows where our heads have been spending time.

When talking to my friend, what frightened and surprised me the most was my response. I sounded so broken and hopeless! I just didn't realize until I heard myself speaking. Have you ever been in one of those conversations when what you say comes out in slow motion? Well, in hearing it said back to me, I realized the trouble I was in for spilling just how hopeless I was.

I do remember saying, "Really? I say that? I didn't realize I said I don't like a lot of what I do."

My friend then asked me, "What would you like to do? If Christy could do what she wanted, what would that be?"

"Huh." I heard her; I just needed to get my thoughts together to respond without feeling so much guilt. Even hearing those words made me feel that I was betraying myself, and everyone else, just for being asked the questions.

"Well," I said, "I don't really know. I don't think like that. I don't like to think or talk about options that aren't options."

Well, there it was! If I'd sounded hopeless before, now I sounded really hopeless! When I think about what I really felt, I know it was guilt; guilt for thinking, let alone feeling, that there were some things in my life that didn't seem fair. I knew that some of the changes I felt God wanted to do in me would surprise many, including myself. I was confused about why I would want to change something that was fruitful – if God was blessing something, why would I want to change it? Most leaders would die for what I get to do, so to complain about it made me feel so guilty that I shut down any potential idea of change; I had it good, and God had blessed me greatly.

I thought: How stupid is that? I get to do amazing things. I lead an amazing church. I preach and teach around the world. I have the most incredible friends around the planet. So how the heck did I get here? How did I even say what I just said?

But there I was spilling about just how unhappy I was with areas of my life, and as I thought through that conversation with my friend it became clear to me that I had believed things about myself that weren't true. I had areas in my mind where I had believed some things were never going to change. In fact, I had never even allowed myself to believe that I had any options. To me it was no different than if I wanted to play professional football! It wasn't an option, so why even bother talking about it?

This had become a weak area for me. We all deal with our weaknesses differently. For myself, instead of thinking about the things that I wished were different, and the possibility of changing them, I just chose to focus on what was happening at the time. I rarely thought about those areas of disappointment and if I did, I would just go back to the same pattern of putting my head down and focusing on whatever I was currently facing. What I thought of as strength as I continued to press on had gradually developed into more like a slow death in parts of my soul. I had, unknowingly, shut down in different ways. If we shut down physically, obviously we die. But there are all kinds of death. It's why we live among the walking dead. We are body, soul, and spirit, and God works change in all three areas of our lives. If we're only alive in one or two areas, then we're only partially alive.

We have to remember that when God is trying to get our attention, it's not to scold, but to give us more of Himself. Sometimes we misunderstand God's invitation to change. But this God moment with my friend had moved my heart to realize some things that I needed to be able to see. I didn't understand all of it at the time, because when God's moving on my heart, it sometimes takes my head a while to catch up.

If, as Paul said, the children of God will be led by the Spirit of God, this means there will be times when our spirit man is leading us into the purposes of God, and our mind has to catch up with where God's Spirit is leading us. We are not to be led by our thoughts; we are led by God's Spirit. It's also why God sometimes leads us in a way that we can't make sense of in the natural:

1. Paul tells us that one of the ways that we yield to God is by submitting to Him in worship. The mind hates rest and it fights submission. To submit to God is to worship God. When we are worshipping God, we are in fact submitting to His Lordship. A transformed life begins on the path of worship. We redirect that area of our mind in worship to God, dwelling on good things, and feeding it with the traits we desire to produce. When we are submitting our thought life to God, we are protecting our most important asset.

   The Bible tells us time and again that we have responsibility to guard our heart and guard our mind. This is to be an intentional responsibility.

2. The mind needs a focus. If I am going to set a goal for my life about something I would like to change, I need a visual. I need to know where I am at, and where I need to go. If I want to lose weight, I don't put a picture of a pig on my fridge. That's not my goal. Hopefully!

3. The mind needs to be fed. What you feed your mind on is what you become.

So much of the time we don't live free because we're not feeding ourselves on the right things. Proverbs 18:15 tells us, "The mind of a smart person is ready to get knowledge. The wise person listens to learn more" (ICB).

It's not that we don't have access to the things of God, but rather we don't take the time to know, or consider, the responsibility to feed our minds the right stuff.

When I was growing up, my dad would often say to us, "garbage in, garbage out". It's impossible to feed ourselves the wrong things and live in freedom. You cannot put your hand in the candy jar and pull out an apple.

WHERE YOU DRAW FROM IS WHAT WILL GET PRODUCED IN YOUR LIFE.

What we spend time watching and listening to affects us way more than we realize. If you want to live free you must be intentional with what you are feeding your mind. Proverbs 15:14 says, "A wise person is hungry for knowledge, while the fool feeds on trash" (NLT).

No matter how you justify or rationalize it, trash is trash. Sometimes we even negotiate over our trash, believing that at least our trash is cleaner than other people's. At other times we try to justify ourselves, making excuses like, "It could be worse." Yet God says that if we feed ourselves trash, the things of this world – trash TV, trash movies, trash magazines, and trash video games – then we are being foolish. No matter how you justify it you cannot feed yourself trash and expect your mind to be healthy. **And if your mind isn't healthy, you are not healthy!**

God is inviting us into change, but in order to change, we have to feed ourselves the proper nutrition. This is what it looks like to live intentionally. As believers we're not meant to just have a "whatever" attitude: I'll just think about whatever comes across my mind, I will just play it by ear, and hopefully I will grow in my walk with God. We must be intentional by what we choose to feed our mind with.

Harvard did a study years ago about the mind, about thinking, and they concluded that the more long-term someone thinks, the more successful they are in life. People who don't do well are those who are only thinking about today, thinking about the here and now, and what's best for them. God wants you to be successful. God wants you to be great. God wants you to grow. But God also wants you to be hungry for the right things.

FEEDING OURSELVES ON THE TRUTH OF WHO GOD IS, AND WHAT GOD SAYS, IS WHAT FEEDS OUR DESIRE FOR THE RIGHT THINGS.

Our interactions with God are acts of worship, where we choose to submit to the One greater than ourselves. When we meditate on God's word it transforms us from the inside out. Another word for meditation actually means resounding musical sound. To meditate on the things of God is an act of worship as we submit to Him and relinquish control.

Living from God's truth does not happen by accident, but rather by choosing daily to meditate on what God says. God's desire for you is the same. He not only wants to heal you, but to keep you healed. God is not just moving what's not working into another area of our house (our lives), but rather He is completely wanting to renovate, to remove everything from the house all together.

The truth of God's word in us not only leads us into freedom, but keeps us there. James explains the importance of meditating on, and continuing in, this truth:

> They see their faces and then go away and quickly forget what they looked like. But the truly happy people are those who carefully study God's perfect law that makes people free, and they continue to study it. They do not forget what they heard, but they obey what God's teaching says. Those who do this will be made happy.
>
> (James 1:24–25 NCV)

Live and meditate on the truth of what God has said about you. If we adjust, dilute, or mess with any of God's truth, we mess with our freedom.

One of the ways that I can tell if I am growing in God's Word is by how fast I am able to recognize the enemy's lies. Ask yourself, how quickly do you recognize truth? How quickly do you realize the enemy is lying to you? How long does it take you to know what God says about you compared to what the world says? This will reveal how much of God's truth is inside you.

This invitation to the renovated mind is a journey we will all be on until we're with Jesus. We have to make the daily choices that lead us, and keep us, in freedom. This is a lifestyle; from when you get up in the morning, as an act of worship, you are going before your God: "I have set the Lord continually before me; Because He is at my right hand, I will not be shaken" (Psalm 16:8 NASB), until you go to bed: "When I remember You on my bed, I meditate on You in the night watches" (Psalm 63:6 NASB).

I have found that the journey and process have been nothing like I thought they would be. But if you want it, you'll make the time for it.

Pastorally, I have learned to recognize when someone is really ready for change, because they make it clear by their commitment that no matter how uncomfortable it gets they will stick with it. If you want to change, you have to not only decide that you want it, but that no matter how uncomfortable it gets you will still commit yourself to the process. We become whatever we commit ourselves to.

THE COMMITMENTS YOU MAKE WILL DEVELOP OR DESTROY YOU, BUT EITHER WAY THEY DEFINE YOU.

Begin to ask the Lord about your commitments; ask Him to reveal to you where your mind is spending time. What are you focusing on, meditating on, and thinking about? Ask yourself how often you take your thoughts back to God for Him to review. I know this: if you ask the Lord to begin to speak to you about your thought life, you will see things that you didn't even realize were affecting the way you are living.

THE MIND IS NOT TO BE MASTERED; IT IS TO COME UNDER THE SUBMISSION
AND THE LORDSHIP OF JESUS CHRIST.

As you bring your mind, your thought life, and your actions to the Lord, allow Him to reveal and heal the way you think. The more you allow God to heal the way you think, the more you will encounter Him and realize He has more for you. I am learning that just when I think I know how kind God is towards me, He is waiting to extend more than even my idea of what more actually is. There is always more than enough and as long as you continue to say "yes" to God's invitation, He will continue to do far beyond what you even thought was possible. Enjoy the journey, as there is healing in the joy God sets before us in bringing about more of His healing into our lives.

CHAPTER 7

Identity: who do you think you are?

The most secure are those who know whom they belong to, not allowing what they see, or what they go through, to determine who they become.

So many people feel as if they are often overlooked, discounted, or even worthless. There is often an oppressive worry of feeling "different" or being left out. Why does society think that some people have everything, yet treat others as if they were nothing? People worry: everyone gets chosen except me. Why is that? Am I less of a person than others? Will I be left out? If others aren't better than me then why do they get picked and I get overlooked? So many people feel this great pressure and confusion. We all have an identity, yet many wrestle it. This idea of who we are, or who we are meant to be, is a real struggle. It feels like the junior high playground sometimes, where everyone gets picked but us. People wake up every day feeling overwhelmed, walking aimlessly throughout life, breathing, but not really living for anything.

The enemy is fully aware of our concerns, questions, and struggles about identity, and he feeds the fear of being overlooked, or that God has chosen to use everyone except us. One thing we can count on is that the enemy will always go after our identity. Why you? Why would God pick you? Why would anyone want to marry you? Why would anyone ever listen to you? Why should you get to lead? Why should you get to pray for people? Why should you get to teach? Why should God entrust you with anything? Don't you know how messed up you are?

WHO YOU THINK YOU ARE, AND WHY GOD WOULD WANT TO USE YOU, ARE ONGOING QUESTIONS THAT THE ENEMY — AND EVEN WELL-MEANING PEOPLE — WILL CONSTANTLY CONFRONT YOU WITH.

We are called not to just exist; we're called to make a difference.

AS LONG AS WE HAVE BREATH WE HAVE AN ASSIGNMENT FROM GOD.

It doesn't make any sense to exist for no reason. God has created us with purpose and meaning. Just as with anyone who makes something, it is the creator who knows the reason for what they have made.

Why would the enemy spend so much time going after who we are? Why does the enemy often haunt and taunt us with feelings of unworthiness? We've talked about mercy and worship and God transforming us from the inside out, but why do all of these things matter so much? Why are we focusing on the inside of who we are; why are we trying to remember what God has said to us and done for us? Could it be that the enemy tends to accuse us in the area of worth so we will spend more time feeling like we have to prove who we are, rather than living in the freedom of what God has already said is true?

Of course God has placed us here to be a part of something bigger than ourselves. It wouldn't make any sense otherwise. It doesn't make any sense to be created for nothing. But **what we do as part of the bigger picture first has to be established in who we are.** Identity is a distraction for many, even for believers. And sadly there are those who are too embarrassed to say they are struggling or confused because they think that if they believe in God, they should know better. But if we ignore or refuse to acknowledge these areas, then we won't be able to change them. Freedom always takes place when our struggle has come into the light, where it can be worked on with clarity.

We belong to God. We've been bought with a high price for a reason, and the reason is love. We are loved by God, and from this place of being loved we are then able to love others. We are loved to love. That is our main call and our main assignment. Little matters more than love. Love is why we've been created, and one day we will stand before God and give an account for how we lived, and how we loved: How well did we love God and how did we love our neighbors?

NO MATTER WHAT WE DO, LOVE IS TO BE THE FOUNDATION THAT LEADS TO OUR WHY.

This is why I don't believe the most important question is "How much do we love God?", but rather, "Do we know how much God loves us?" We are loved to love. We cannot do what we're made for unless we first know that we are born in love, and born to love. When we know we're loved and accepted, and when we know God is always with us, then the fear of being bypassed, forgotten, or overlooked has no room within us. However, if we confuse our identity, we then confuse our calling. Knowing what we're made for, and what we're supposed to be doing with our life, always stems from knowing first who and whose we are. This is why when the apostle Paul addresses knowing God's will for our lives, he starts with remembering what God has done for us: "God demonstrates His own love for us in this: While we were still sinners, Christ died for us" (Romans 5:8).

THIS ISN'T ABOUT YOU GETTING YOUR LIFE TOGETHER SO YOU CAN WORK FOR GOD; THIS IS ABOUT YOU BEING LOVED BY GOD.

More than anything else, God wants you to know how well you are loved. The value of something always gets revealed by the price one is willing to pay to obtain it. Jesus paid the highest price for you – His own life – because to Him your value exceeds anything else. This is love. The sacrifice paid reveals the depth of the love.

When love is exposed it reveals the deeper desire of purpose. God's love for you is that you would walk in the confidence of who you are, firmly planted in Him, in His image, as the pinnacle of His Creation. The greatest love has been given, one life for another, so that you might live in love, but also in hope, calling, and purpose.

Receiving revelation about what we are here for must always come after being secure in the revelation of our true identity. Who are we? Why do our lives matter? Why does the enemy want us to question ourselves over and over? Because if we don't know who we are, then how do we know that what we are doing with our life is in fact the very thing we have been made to do? The enemy is fully aware of our insecurities when it comes to our identity, which is why he loves to attack us in this area. Remember, he forgot who he was and thought more of himself than he should have, and that resulted in him being shot out of heaven faster than lightning.

A MISPLACED IDENTITY CAN NOT ONLY HAUNT US, IT CAN MISDIRECT OUR PURPOSE.

The enemy will always undermine one of the greatest gifts God has given us, and that is the knowledge that God chose us. No one is a mistake. God chose to create us and design us "in His image". Just think about that for a minute. God could have created us in any image, yet He chose to bring us into the intimacy of Himself. Putting all of Himself on the table, so to speak. Then we can always remember that we were not a "guess" or a "simple idea" or an "afterthought", but rather purposely made by the Great Creator!

When we live outside of our true identity, we live with a poverty mentality. A poverty mindset isn't just a fear of lacking finances; it can involve any area of our life where we don't fully trust God to provide for us. Many people struggle with a poverty mindset, whether it is to do with believing we are created by God, loved by Him, or called into purpose.

In traveling the world, one of the questions I get asked a thousand times over is, "How do I know what God's called me to? How do I know His will for my life, or if I am doing what He wants?" My response is always the same. Before you ask about knowing God's will, are you clear about who you are? Of course it is important that we know what we are called to, but if we don't first have our identity firmly placed in Christ, our calling becomes inconsistent and irrelevant. Millions of people around the world are busy going to school or making a lot of money, many are even doing their best to make the world around them a better place, yet deep inside they are left unfulfilled. Yes it's true, even making lots of money, solving problems, or serving your country can still leave emptiness if you don't understand who you are. Knowing to whom you belong, and why you are alive, are the questions that lie deep within every soul, waiting to be answered.

THIS IS WHY OUR DESTINY – BEING LOVED AND CREATED BY GOD – ALWAYS PRECEDES CALLING. CALLING CAN CHANGE THROUGHOUT THE YEARS, BUT GOD'S LOVE FOR US WILL NEVER CHANGE.

From the beginning of our lives when God formed us (see Psalm 139), it has never been just for "the now", but for the whole of eternity. It reveals how much thought God has put into your life. God has placed eternity into our hearts. The book of Ecclesiastes tells us that life is not just about what we do here on earth, but it's about more than that, it's about eternity. More than anything else, this is what the enemy will go after. Living with this life in mind is not only not how were wired, it's also disillusioning. Dr. Martyn Lloyd-Jones has a great reminder of this in saying, "When men forget the next world and concentrate only on this present life, this world becomes a kind of living hell."

Sometimes we get so short-sighted, even in the church, that we forget to think and live with eternity in mind. It's also why, in the coming years, I don't imagine that the main struggle in the church will be about what gifting we have, but rather it will be centered in the deeper issue of identity.

If the enemy can keep you and me, and those we love, in a place where we forget who we are, we will become complacent in our most important roles. Knowing who we are is foundational to remembering why we are. Who we are always answers the why and what of our lives. Things around us will change. Your life will change, the world will change, but who you are in Christ is a firm deal. It is solid, and no one can take this truth from you unless you allow them to.

It has been a great sadness to watch how much trauma and tragedy have taken place around the world in the last few years. But to watch the church's response, many times responding from fear, and even adjusting the Bible according to the culture, has been very discouraging at times. Sadly, and hopefully I am wrong, I believe that we will see even more of this in the coming years.

THE GREATER THE PRESSURE ON OUR OWN LIVES, THE MORE OUR WEAK AREAS WILL BE EXPOSED.

It is vital we remember who we are, why we are here and, most importantly, that our anchor must be found in Christ alone. This is where we are called to live from. Your world might shake a little, but remember that you serve an unshakable God who holds everything and is fully aware of it all. That should give great security. The most secure are those who know whom they belong to, not allowing what they see, or what they go through, to determine who they become. Each of us must live in this truth.

If we, as the church, are unsure of our identity, we are not going to be much support for the world around us. Our struggles and hardships, loves and losses, even our sexuality, are not our identity. Our identity is found in Christ alone. If God doesn't define you, then others will do it for you.

IF GOD DOESN'T DEFINE YOU, WHAT YOU DO WILL DEFINE YOU; OR THE SEASON THAT YOU ARE IN, OR WHAT YOU ARE FACING, WHOM YOU ARE DATING, OR EVEN WHAT YOU STRUGGLE WITH, CAN BE THE FORCE THAT SCREAMS WITHIN YOU: "THIS IS WHO YOU ARE! THIS IS YOUR IDENTITY."

We make our identity up out of all sorts of the wrong things: we think that how we have sex is our identity, whom we love is our identity, our looks, our ministry, our family, our job. It's a shaky and faulty foundation to stand upon, not to mention it only produces insecurity. It's also why the fear of change within a relationship or career has caused many people to feel like they are losing themselves.

IF YOUR IDENTITY IS FOUND IN ANYTHING OTHER THAN CHRIST, WHEN THOSE THINGS SHIFT OR CHANGE, AS THEY SURELY WILL, YOU WILL FEEL AS IF YOU ARE LOSING YOUR MIND, YOUR SECURITY, AND YOUR IDENTITY, BECAUSE IT HAS BEEN IN THE WRONG PLACE.

Over the years I have seen this happen, when people have put all that they are into their job, or their ministry, or their kids, or a relationship, and then when it has changed, their whole world has fallen apart.

I have had to walk through this myself a few different times and it's never been easy. When my husband's father, John Wimber, passed away in 1997 our whole world changed overnight, literally. We had both grown up in the Vineyard Movement, both worked at Vineyard Ministries and at Vineyard Music, we both attended the same churches we had attended our entire lives, and when John died everything changed.

People who we thought loved us, and were "for us", as Sean and Christy, changed overnight. Where we worked had changed because John was such a driving force, and really the visionary and protector of the ministries. Our church had already gone through massive change as the pastor had derailed (and not just once), so we had just had a new guy come in to lead our home church. There was not a day where there were not new changes to our existing life which we had invested in so deeply. I remember being at work, standing in the coffee break room being in shock, when two days after John died someone came and asked me to clean out his office.

People's real agendas came to the forefront quickly, and to be honest I think we were a bit in shock for some time, as more and more heartbreaking realizations came that we were forced to walk through. It felt like we weren't just grieving the loss of a father, but grieving a massive change in what had been a major part of our lives. There was not a day for a very long season where we didn't have to grieve what used to be. Everything had changed on every level, and most of it was very hurtful. People had no idea what was happening to us or what we had to put up with (and don't even to this day), but even during those painful times I remember where the Lord kept saying to me, "Christy, remember how this feels so you never make others feel how you feel right now." I had to make this choice over and over again. As I look back, all our securities were lost, and the only thing that lasted was what was real in our relationship with God. Everything else fell away. But it was in this place where God's redefinition of who we were in Him, and the daily choices to trust Him in spite of what we saw or had to walk through, are the things which have outlasted everything else. We had to trust God as we went forward day by day.

Slowly, God defined us and cared for us in deep ways, which protected and sustained us into where we are, and who we are, now, but realizing our true identity has been a process; a process I still find myself in at times. There are many false belief systems about ministry.

THE MINISTRY WILL NOT CARE FOR YOU ONCE IT'S GONE. NO MATTER HOW BIG A MINISTRY IS, IT WILL COME AND GO.

Nothing is forever, and no matter how many great things come out of it, the ministry cannot be the foundation of our identity.

One of the many things I learned through losing so much was to "hold on to things loosely". In other words, your world is going to change. What you're doing today, even leading and serving, will not be forever. So focus on strengthening who you are in Christ, and then when things change, instead of it destroying you, you will find that even in the midst of change your identity is reinforced in God.

This is where I believe the Scripture that says God has the power to work everything out for good for those who love Him. If we focus on loving God, and being loved by Him, then somehow, in some way, God will make good come out of our most difficult of transitions. In His sovereignty, God has designed our lives so that relationship in Him, and with Him, is always the main purpose.

So yes, of course life will change. Your jobs will come and go. Your kids will grow up, move out, and get on with their lives – even though I wish I could pin my kids down forever, it's not the way it works! Areas where you have invested your life may turn out differently to how you planned. Things will get shaken, or will change, and it's only when our identity is firmly planted in Christ that we can live in the freedom that no matter the change, we can rest in the truth that not only is God with us, He is working out how good will come about.

What does it look like to be "made in God's image"?

The Bible tells us that "God created mankind in his own image, in the image of God he created them; male and female he created them" (Genesis 1:27).

At the core of our identity is the fact that we are children of God: male and female, made in His image. We are not in competition with Him, or with others. If we forget this truth, we can easily find ourselves living from the wrong place, and produce the wrong things. One of which is that we will always feel as if we have to compete with others wherever God has placed us.

Through Jesus, we have been justified through a just act, by a just God. We must remember His mercy, worship Him in our choices and how we live, and honor Him by yielding to the ongoing sanctification of God making us more like Him. We must keep our focus and faith on Him. "In Christ" is who we are, and in Him we must remain. We are His church, His children, His bride. I don't think we talk enough about the church being the bride of Christ. It is amazing to think about: God chose us. It was His decision to make us His bride. There is nothing more attractive than a bride on her wedding day. There is something really beautiful about attending a wedding where the bride knows that she is looked upon and loved. She knows that everyone is there to see her beauty, and to see her express her love for her groom.

This beauty and love that everyone desires often brings tears to our eyes and stirs our emotions. But can you imagine how it would be if the bride felt ugly? What if she thought she looked fat, and that all the guests were coming to compare her to other brides? What if the bride was gossiping, bad-mouthing and mocking her bridesmaids as she walked down the aisle? What if she didn't lift her face because of shame or embarrassment, and if all the people who had gathered to see her special day were not allowed to look at the beauty of her face? This would not make sense, yet how often do we live like this as the church, before Jesus, our Groom?

If we think about how our God could have chosen us to be anything – yet He chose us to be His bride. No groom picks an ugly bride. Every bride is beautiful on her wedding day, especially to her groom. The bride has been chosen. Out of everyone, he has chosen her. He wants her. He is proud of her.

WE OFTEN FORGET WHO WE ARE AS THE BRIDE OF CHRIST, AND THE POWER OF BEING CHOSEN.

We have to learn to celebrate the beauty of the fullness and diversity of His bride, without feeling threatened that it will take value away from our part in the body of Christ. As well as being His bride, we are also His body. I don't slap myself in the face because my eyes are pretty! I care for my face. Stupid, but a rather funny example of what our behavior is like when we feel threatened by other parts of the body, instead of realizing that they are in fact extensions of the same body that make us whole, that complete us.

Someone else's beauty and gifting should cause us to celebrate each other, just as it reveals our Creator.

IT SHOULD NOT CAUSE FEAR THAT WE WILL NOT BE CHOSEN, BECAUSE WE HAVE ALREADY BEEN CHOSEN. IT SHOULD NOT CAUSE FEAR THAT WE ARE NOT GOOD ENOUGH, BECAUSE GOD HAS ALREADY SAID WE ARE. IT SHOULD NOT CAUSE FEAR THAT WE WON'T HAVE A PLACE, BECAUSE THE GROOM HAS GIVEN US HIMSELF.

If we begin to question the choice of the Groom, then we undermine His choice. If God picks us, then no one can say that we are not enough – not even ourselves! There is no one like you, and there is no one like the person next to you. Both need to be celebrated. As Janis Joplin said, "Don't compromise yourself, you are all you've got."

WHEN WE COMPROMISE, OR ALLOW OURSELVES TO OPERATE OUTSIDE OF THE IMAGE OF OUR CREATOR, THAT IS WHEN WE START TO MAKE CHOICES OUTSIDE OF WHO WE WERE CALLED TO BE.

Knowing and being secure in who we are is what leads us into all that we are destined for.

THE REVELATION OF GOD COMES FROM THE PLACE OF INTIMACY IN OUR RELATIONSHIP WITH HIM. IT IS IN THIS PLACE THAT HE DEFINES US, REFINES US, AND REMINDS US WHAT WE ARE HERE FOR.

This is the place where our identity is made secure. The enemy will always attack our identity, because if we forget who we are, we begin to live for all the wrong reasons. If we forget who we are, then insecurity, jealousy, and competition can find a home in us. If we are fully secure in the Lord, and in our relationship with Him, then we will be secure in everything else. When we are secure in Christ, other options and our old ways of living aren't attractive any more.

The Bible says, "Taste and see that the Lord is good" (Psalm 34:8). Once we taste of the Lord, nothing else tastes as good. Nothing else satisfies. But if we allow our taste buds to go outside, we begin to grapple with the enticements of this world, and we become unstable. Instability produces insecurity, and we start to question our identity. If Christ is not our center, we will look for other ways to find our identity and security, because we were made for purpose, made to be used, to make a difference. Living from the wrong place feeds our flesh and its desire for the wrong things. When we know that we are living below our birthright in Christ, we again empower the enemy to torture our minds with the question, who do we think we are?

Why do we feel the need to work so hard to make things happen? Why do we worry that if we don't make it happen, then no one will? This is not just about saying "no" to sin, but rather feeling safe and secure **that the God who has designed us is also the God who will make a way for us. When we empower insecurity, it is just a sign we have forgotten whom we belong to. Everyone has insecurities, but if we live from that place of a forgotten or misplaced identity, we will begin to work and strive for what we already have.** In Christ is where we find mercy, hope, joy, peace, and rest, but also our sure identity. We know that God not only will take care of us, but also has a plan for us. If insecurity is empowered, it often produces the need to stay busy, and make success happen in our life, or to make sure that it doesn't happen in other people's lives. We live in a world where the need for success, and the need to be "relevant", has crept into the church. When insecurity isn't dealt with, it produces competition, which fights for power in the wrong way and with the wrong motives. Competition opens the door to jealousy, and vice versa.

JEALOUSY NOT ONLY STEALS OUR PEACE, BUT IT KILLS DESTINY. JEALOUSY FORGETS WHO WE ARE AND WHAT WE HAVE.

If we start to look at others and fight for something that is not ours, not only does it take us off course, but it also slowly kills the areas in which we ourselves are called to be powerful. It's a distraction from our own identity. When we are so busy looking at others, then we have no time to focus on what God is doing within us. It's a great reminder that to live in Christ is to stand firm in where God has you. Staying in our lane is vital to our own health and growth.

WHEN YOU KNOW WHO YOU ARE, YOU DON'T WANT TO BE ANYONE ELSE.

George MacDonald wrote:

> I would rather be what God chose to make me than the most glorious creature that I could think of; for to have been thought about, born in God's thought, and then made by God, is the dearest, grandest and most precious thing in all thinking.

There is no one else like you. There is no one who can do what you do in the way that God has designed you to do it. Celebrate the fact that God has chosen you. Celebrate the gifts and calling God has placed within you as you have been a part of His plan all along. You are part of His plan and everything you do is a part of God's bigger plan. To think that the great God of all Creation has chosen you, has designed you, but has also called you, should rock you to the core of how deeply you are loved. There is no one before you or after you who can do or be what your Creator has created specially, just for you. Just think on that for a while…

CHAPTER 8

What is grace in the twenty-first century?

The more that we – as the church – understand the power of grace to us, the more effective we will be in carrying grace to the world around us. We cannot give out of what we ourselves do not have. This is not a sermon to be preached, this is a lifestyle we must learn to cultivate.

We will look at grace in calling and how God's grace confirms His call within us, but first, what does grace given to ourselves and others in everyday life look like in the church? Before we talk about grace to the world around us, we must address the grace "God has given to each of us" (Ephesians 4:7 VOICE).

I believe grace needs to be redefined. Grace has become a sort of buffet mentality approach where it has a different meaning to different people within the church family.

Grace, I've found, is often misunderstood. Some worry that if grace is shown then people will take advantage, while others believe that because grace is free, there are endless amounts to be used up. Neither attitude is healthy. Grace is not to be approached with a watered-down, nonchalant attitude where I can do whatever I want because at the end of the day God will forgive me tomorrow. But neither is grace to be withheld and only given to those whom we deem worthy to receive it.

WE ARE NOT THE ONES TO DECIDE WHO IS WORTHY OF GRACE. WE CAN ONLY DECIDE IF WE WILL RECEIVE GRACE FOR OURSELVES, AND IF WE WILL EXTEND IT TO OTHERS.

Learning about the grace of God has been a process for me in my walk with God. In fact, it has been one of the weak areas in my own life. When it came to church life the environment was rather laid-back, where gifts and power had greater influence than character. Over the years I have learned the importance of character, yet I feel like I am still learning, almost playing catch-up, because this wasn't an area I was equipped in. When it came to knowing the Bible, it was really only the Scriptures that my dad had taught us on Sunday nights – if we remembered what church had been about then we would get an ice cream, a great incentive in my early years. But even more so, it is the Scriptures I learned early on in the Quaker Church, sitting on those tiny Sunday school chairs, which I still remember to this day.

My own journey of learning about the Bible, and what it looks like to follow hard after Christ, has really come later in my life. I have learned different things from different people who God has sent across my path at important times, or when I needed to grow up in certain areas. I have had amazing people in my life, yet even still, one thing I knew was that when it came to church leadership, it wasn't what I wanted to do with my life.

The fear of the poor character of leaders (some family aside) drove me away from wanting to lead anything visibly in church. I am making a broad generalization here, but there were enough elders and pastors in my church who lived one way in front of the congregation, and another way at home. That's just the way it was. My friends and I would joke about it, but we honestly thought that was how it was meant to be. We used to laugh about one man in particular who would swear at us and then pick up his guitar to lead worship in small group. He was horrible to his family, yet he was an "elder" and even though his importance was much smaller than he portrayed when he talked about it, he was still an elder within our church and he was still in leadership.

This has been something I've had to work out, because I was always confused about the double life. Of course, it wasn't everyone, but enough people to bring me to the point where I didn't want much to do with it. Why would these people call themselves "spiritual leaders"? What exactly did this mean? As I got older and started leading things myself, I began to question why those things in my history of the church were even allowed. Why would the leaders empower these people, and also, who would want that stuff released over their church or ministry? Didn't we care how dishonest they were with their lifestyle? I wish it was only a few people, but even in writing this, name after name comes to mind. The whispers of those who had affairs, those who were physically abusive to their kids, a baby born out of wedlock to a married pastor, an elder who was sleeping with his daughter – for years. There was one pastor who was living a double life and had a second family in another country. I was really good friends with his son, who refused to ever set foot in a church again after he found out what his dad had done. Tragic stories of leaders' choices and what those choices did to their worlds around them. I call them "kingdom casualties", and they are everywhere.

My history is not unlike a lot of church history, because sadly, as with anything else, there are unhealthy things in all churches and movements, and there are weak areas which always need to be addressed. We often see successful churches and movements and create an idealism, even nostalgia, in believing that those days were better than they actually were. **Nostalgia can be crippling, especially to the following generations of the church.** Every church and every movement is a reminder that even when God uses broken people, and many incredible things have taken place, it does not mean that all is good or healthy. It is not a picture of perfection, but rather a reminder of the goodness and the grace of God. However, I do believe there is great accountability to learn from one generation to the next. Each church and movement has great abilities and giftings, but each also carries its own blind spots and weaknesses. If they are addressed, God's mercy can use those areas to produce an even greater story of power and redemption. However, if ignored, they do incredible amounts of damage.

From what I was exposed to, and from those who caused so much damage, how refreshing it would be to hear just one of these people talk about the need to work on their inner life and character, rather than their Facebook page and who is endorsing them now. How great it would be to hear that one of them was spending time repairing their family, and was stacking chairs on Sundays in a church where nobody knew who they were. I have never understood why the platform was even an option for them any more. Didn't they lose that privilege?

What I think about today is not those who failed but the many who have been so wounded by how the church has handled, or mishandled, various situations. The wake is great.

WHAT SURPRISES ME IS NOT THE FACT THAT PEOPLE MAKE BAD CHOICES, BUT RATHER THE RESPONSE OF THE CHURCH.

On more than a few occasions I have had to speak up to question why the public platform would be given to people who have a track record of unhealthy choices, accusations, and fruit that is not spiritual. The response has been not only confusing but sadly disappointing. I have been told on numerous occasions I was unforgiving, a person who lacked grace, and some even called me a Pharisee. And for years I believed it. I believed I was being judgmental, and it caused a deep hesitancy in me, where I questioned myself because of the check in my own spirit. I now realize that much of what I've seen and been told is nonsense, but that in itself is a journey of grace.

I HAVE COME TO REALIZE GOD'S GRACE HAS PROTECTED ME, NOT FROM THE WORLD, BUT FROM THE LACK OF HEALTHY LEADERSHIP WITHIN THE CHURCH.

All actions have consequences, and my question has always been: "When grace is needed, especially when there has been failure, who exactly are we having grace towards?"

I often wonder what kind of grace we are showing, because we tend to talk about grace in terms of the perpetrators, but what about their victims? What about those who have been hurt, damaged, or even destroyed by the consequences? Where is the grace for them? I am completely for grace being offered to all, but grace is no good if it's not given to all involved in any given situation. What about those kingdom casualties I mentioned? We are quick to hand out second, third, fourth chances, but we mustn't forget those who were violated. I haven't often seen grace given to those families who were affected by another's immorality, or those victims of the ones who have chosen to make poor choices. The children who have been abandoned by their parents, the churches left reeling by a leader's fall, even those who have given up on church because they have seen its inconsistencies – where is our grace for them? Where have all these kingdom casualties ended up?

SO IS GRACE ONLY GRACE WHEN IT'S GIVEN TO THE PERSON WHO CONTINUALLY WALKS IN SIN?

Perhaps we do need to redefine grace. What does grace mean in the twenty-first century?

See, with "the grace given" that Paul talks about in Romans 12, there is a responsibility that follows. The fact that God would use ordinary, broken human beings as vessels of His grace, and delight in it, is awe-inspiring. He's proud of how His grace is beating through your imperfect-but-redeemed life, and through the church. I mean that's what Ephesians 3:10–11 is all about. But we also have responsibility to understand the difference between the restoring power of Jesus and the right to a position.

There is always restoration, of course – that is the gospel – but we have to ask, what is it restoration to, and does it have to be something visible?

Surely we cannot divorce our personal lives from our spiritual lives using grace as an excuse?

Paul claims that grace being lived out is founded in sacrificial living. Grace at its core is not something to be used or abused for our own selfish ambition, but is to rest in the peace of knowing that God is with us, for us, and gives us the power to be able to live right. We see ourselves clearly, but also our Father clearly, who is good, generous, and loving, and invites us to serve His purposes. Grace is empowered by having a healthy picture of who we are, and who God is. Any time that I have encountered the power of God, it's given me a clear perspective of who I am, but also who I am not. I almost always walk away with a sober reminder, a healthy fear of the Lord, where again I am called to the place of worship to the God who is on the throne, and that I must never forget my place.

A healthy fear of the Lord seems to be missing in today's culture. It is not a fear that causes us to shrink back or hide from God, but rather it reveals our deepest need to be with Him, and the awe we have for Him and His greatness. A healthy fear of the Lord will always cause us to see how magnificent He is, and will keep us grounded in the place where we would never want to take advantage of His grace. We need to ask ourselves: "Where is my fear of God?" We have gone so far away from the "hellfire and brimstone" teaching that hell is rarely spoken about now. In fact, hell is more often used as a cuss word than a destination. I can't remember when I last heard the gospel preached and hell was discussed as being real. More and more, I hear people avoiding talking about it in case of causing offense. The approach is generally more along the lines of loving people into the kingdom, and a focus on grace, which I completely agree with to a degree. But if our goal as the church is to reach people for Christ, then we must offer all of who Christ is. He is love, He is peace, He is life, He is hope; but He is also the righteous judge. **It is unloving to only offer the parts of Christ that we feel comfortable with, and at the same time, it is devaluing something most valuable when we lower the standard in order to reach the culture.** Jesus never lowered His standards when He was loving, reaching out to, and completely changing, the culture around Him.

I do agree with the idea of loving people into the kingdom, but equally I believe it is unloving to not tell the truth about hell. The gospel is offensive. It offends in order to reveal; the true message of the gospel reveals the depth of our human sin, and the reality that without Christ we have nothing, we are nothing. With that understanding, we fall more in love with Him and the grace extended to us. **We have strayed too far from the gospel being central to our lives and faith if it is now considered judgmental for a leader to remind us of the reality of heaven and hell.** Both are real, and both should be addressed. It is unloving to only address the things we find comfortable.

"And the Word was made flesh, and dwelt among us, (and we beheld his glory, the glory as of the only begotten of the Father,) full of grace and truth" John 1:14 (KJV). To hear about the gospel is to be confronted with the truth. The encouraging truth that we have access to grace, but also the challenging truth of how much we need that grace, as we have fallen short of the goodness of our God. Therefore, as John 1:14 reminds us, to be presented with the grace of God is to be led into truth. Therefore, grace that doesn't lead to truth isn't grace at all. A sign of true grace is where truth is present and therefore freedom is present. Grace and truth work together – grace leads the way, but it is truth that sets us free.

Holding people to a standard that's Scriptural doesn't mean were being unforgiving or judgmental. It means we love them enough to tell them the truth because our desire is that they would live in true freedom.

The grace God gives to us is a precious gift to enable and empower us not only to let go of the past, but also to take hold of our future.

THE GIFT OF GRACE IS JUST THAT – A GIFT. IT IS NOT TO BE TAKEN ADVANTAGE OF, BUT RATHER TREASURED.

I believe the more we treasure the gift of grace to us as the church, the more attractive it will be to the world around us.

Grace to the church

We need grace to the church before we can have grace through the church.

Paul begins to address some of the gifts God uses His people for to serve and love the world. It will be impossible, as it always has been, to serve others, or even to think about others, if we don't live in God's grace. We need it; every day we need it.

But grace is for purpose. In Romans 12:3, Paul says, "For by the grace given me I say to every one of you: Do not think of yourself more highly than you ought, but rather think of yourself with sober judgment." Fully aware that we will operate outside of our own calling, as well as falling into the trap of thinking we are better than another, Paul quickly addresses both of these temptations.

For some of you, your weakness may be to think less of yourself, while others think you're gifted at everything. Neither is true, nor is it helpful to yourself or others.

WHEN YOU DISCOUNT YOURSELF, YOU ARE IN FACT DISCOUNTING GOD WITHIN YOU.

God says you're better than you think, but equally, no one person holds all the gifts. No one person knows everything, and if they think they do then they are no fun to be around! Can you imagine if you could do everything? Not only would you not need anybody else, but you wouldn't be able to get your head through the door!

We need each other, and as the church we will need each other even more in the coming years. We are an army and an army is most effective when its soldiers are fighting for each other, not against. In the battle, we need to understand grace on a deeper level. The distractions of those who choose to say "no" to God will not be the focus in the coming years. People will be desperate for hope and desperate for some resolve, and the Lord is going to get us ready to be the carriers of His grace to those who need it, want it, and are hungry to encounter it.

GOD IS PREPARING HIS BRIDE, AND BEFORE GOD ADDRESSES THE WORLD, HE ALWAYS FIRST ADDRESSES HIS CHURCH.

So how do we treat those who should know better but don't act better? We still show grace. But grace does not mean people can just run over you. Grace does not mean we can do whatever we want to others just because we feel like it. And grace does not mean that our character is secondary to our gifting. To be the church, filled with grace, means we act "with the grace given to us" – how can we not then extend grace to those around us?

A GRACE-FILLED ENVIRONMENT OFFERS A SAFE SPACE, WHERE EVERYONE HAS RESPONSIBILITY FOR THE CHOICES THEY MAKE. HEALTHY ACCOUNTABILITY ALWAYS SURROUNDS SPACES OF GRACE.

I believe we are in a time where the church needs to understand how to have grace for herself. The Bible says, "Therefore, as we have opportunity, let us do good to all people, especially to those who belong to the family of believers" (Galatians 6:10).

Grace is needed everywhere, especially within the church. If the church is to become the safest place for the world, we must first become the safest place for ourselves and each other within the body of Christ. Grace starts with not allowing the weaknesses of others to determine our love for one another. The commitment to grace means commitment to each other, in that as long as we're growing together, and honesty is taking place, we allow people to get well. The power of grace in safety is hugely attractive.

In Acts chapters 2 and 3, we find the power of the first church gathering. Where people shared their lives with each other, giving to those in need, and maturing by listening to those God had placed over them, it was so attractive that even without social media, people were coming to them! People wanted to be a part of what they were doing. This is a picture of grace walked out – where one is lacking, another fills the gap – and it is also a relational picture of true community, and how attractive that is to the world around us.

Loving our leaders

One of the things I am always asking the Lord for is grace in ministry. Many of my friends are those who do the same things that I do, locally and around the world, and we need to change how we treat spiritual leaders generally.

Spiritual leaders need grace just as much as anyone! In our celebrity church culture there is no room for grace for the ones on the stage. What celebrity culture feeds eliminates the space for those who are leading to have areas of brokenness. The illusion that gifted people aren't human is very dangerous and destructive to the church, and to the individual. The trouble is that brokenness doesn't sell, but power does. Weakness is not a popular topic – in fact I've never been invited to speak at an event on the subject of weakness. Power, yes, many times, but never weakness.

This illusion of seeing the stage like a magic pass seems to get confused with perfect people; for some reason people misunderstand and think that church titles create perfect people.

IF WE SET PEOPLE UP AS PERFECT, OR PUT LEADERS UP ON A PEDESTAL, WE SET THEM UP FOR FAILURE. I HAVE WATCHED TOO MANY PEOPLE BLOW UP INSTEAD OF GROW UP BECAUSE THEY WERE PUT ON A PEDESTAL THAT EVENTUALLY GAVE WAY.

Hudson Taylor said that "all God's giants have been weak men, who did great things for God because they reckoned on His being with them". Even when God uses someone powerfully, they are still at best the broken vessel that the apostle Paul wrote about. We must never mistake the vessel for the One who created the vessel. Every role that each person plays this side of heaven matters. The size of the role has never been the point. In fact, we don't get to pick the scope of our lives because God is the One who determines those things.

Even within the church the enemy is quick to use people who, from their own insecurity, do or say things to undermine how God will use you. Don't be on guard waiting for it, but don't be surprised by it either. No matter the stage of influence that God has given you, whether a great or small measure of influence, you must remember that you are human, filled with the Spirit of God, stepping into your call, and by doing so, you are advancing the kingdom of God. Every part matters – it is never the size of what we're doing that matters to God, it is only our "yes" to Him, in obedience, which God is looking for.

Many people whom God calls to step into public ministry are introverts having to take a risk of obedience, and just because they make it look easy, doesn't mean that it is! We actually never really know what it takes for most people to get out of bed and to give their "yes" to God. There has never been a person who has accomplished much for God publicly, who hasn't suffered privately. This is where grace plays such an important role. This is what the early church understood. We must be generous with grace, because none of us know what people go home to at night. At the end of the day, if we want people to show up to do their part, we should be grateful to God for their obedience, and pray that God gives them the grace to walk out what He has called them to.

As someone who preaches to crowds, I understand the power of words. Words are powerful and can be extremely hurtful to the person on the stage, just as words can be extremely hurtful to the person in the audience. We must remember that no matter the role, everyone needs grace in what they're doing. You will need grace in where God calls you, and I will need grace in where God calls me, but if we remember the importance of our words, and if we are gracious to everyone, people are more likely to take more risks in their calling. We do not know how people handle the harsh words of judgment, but we must not think that we can just criticize and abuse people. We can't think that just because someone has a public position they have no feelings – that is deeply unfair, and far too common.

Every person needs space to grow, and to not only give but also receive healing. I would love to see the church become a place where people, leaders included, are able to open up and be free to work towards change and wholeness without fear of being judged by the rest of the church. If we don't allow space with grace for all people, then we cannot expect honesty and true healing to take place. Weakness is not a sign of spiritual immaturity, or a lack of faith. Weakness is a reality – we all have areas of our life which are broken, we all have weak areas, and we must allow all people the space to be honest about these places in them in order for true health to come into the church.

Grace: God's gift from the church to the world

The more that we – as the church – understand the power of grace to us, the more effective we will be in carrying grace to the world around us. We cannot give out of what we ourselves do not have. This is not a sermon to be preached, this is a lifestyle we must learn to cultivate. It is not easy giving grace to people who live differently to us. And it's even more difficult to give grace to people who don't think they are in need of it.

As our culture gets more and more secular, the broken world around us will become more and more obvious. Paul speaks of this as a time of waiting, and groaning, in Romans 8:18–27:

> I consider that our present sufferings are not worth comparing with the glory that will be revealed in us. For the creation waits in eager expectation for the children of God to be revealed. For the creation was subjected to frustration, not by its own choice, but by the will of the one who subjected it, in hope that the creation itself will be liberated from its bondage to decay and brought into the freedom and glory of the children of God. We know that the whole creation has been groaning as in the pains of childbirth right up to the present time. Not only so, but we ourselves, who have the firstfruits of the Spirit, groan inwardly as we wait eagerly for our adoption to sonship, the redemption of

our bodies. For in this hope we were saved. But hope that is seen is no hope at all. Who hopes for what they already have? But if we hope for what we do not yet have, we wait for it patiently. In the same way, the Spirit helps us in our weakness. We do not know what we ought to pray for, but the Spirit himself intercedes for us through wordless groans. And he who searches our hearts knows the mind of the Spirit, because the Spirit intercedes for God's people in accordance with the will of God.

Grace surrounds all of these words from Paul. It is the grace of God which reveals that there will be times when suffering will be present, but that there is also hope, from the truth that suffering will not be forever. The glory of God will make everything you are going through worthwhile. I don't know how, but if God said it, then I do know it's true. Even if it doesn't feel like it, which often it doesn't, the promise of God and Paul's reminder is to encourage us not to get near-sighted, but rather to live our lives in light of the bigger picture of eternity. He also reminds us that not only is there a struggle, but there is a deep groaning in all of us, and everything around us, and until we are with Christ, this groaning will continue.

Even in the midst of this, God wants to encourage us with the reminder that not only is He fully aware of our struggles, but He is right here with us, even praying for us through them! But we cannot force the "redemption of our bodies" (Romans 8:23). We cannot force the world to stop groaning, or play like it is all OK, when God Himself says that this is all part of His plan. What is revealed here in Romans 8 is our deep need for the grace of God.

I wish the church would stop teaching, preaching, writing, and singing about this world becoming more like heaven. This is not heaven. Scripturally, we are not meant to seek heaven, but rather seek the kingdom of God. If we teach that this is heaven, we allow no space for suffering. If we have the power within ourselves to pull heaven into our world, it also places huge pressure on the believer, because if our life isn't looking like heaven, that means we did not pull it into our environment. This produces an idea which is impossible for the believer to carry out.

It eliminates the need for grace in our world. Why would we need grace if this is to be heaven, and everything is getting better and better? Heaven is perfect. This world is not perfect. In heaven there is no brokenness. This world is broken. Each one of us has areas of brokenness that will not be fully liberated from the bondage of decay and brought into His glorious freedom, until we enter eternity (Romans 8:21).

So if this isn't heaven, and the earth and everything in it is groaning, waiting for the redemption of our bodies and all weakness to be made right, then how do we handle this in-between time? Do we ignore those things which don't represent heaven? Do we play like people aren't being martyred for their faith in various parts of the world? How do we handle the areas that aren't fully restored, or fully healed, with the grace God has given to each of us?

WE NEED MORE GRACE THAN WE REALIZE. WE NEED MORE SPACES OF GRACE THAN WE REALIZE.

One of the hardest things for me to figure out in recent years has been when I've seen people receiving ministry at events, because so often the person praying, or the testimony itself, got more attention than the person who was prayed for. The person groaning gets silenced for the popular testimony of what is happening, which sounds more enticing, instead of acknowledging what didn't happen and making that person know that their lack of full restoration isn't their fault at all. It sure has felt like grace was missing.

I can't tell you how many meetings I have sat in, where it has felt like people were trying to out-pray, out-testimony, or outshine each other. The gross competition in healing ministries, where exaggeration is not hard to find and the Bible rarely used, has caused me to rethink my own travel schedule within the last season. "Lord, am I hurting Your church?" has been one of my ongoing prayers. I am a person who loves to see what only God can do best, and that is to encounter people. I love it when God heals; it's a beautiful thing to see, but if we are only giving space to things we feel are more entertaining or exciting, then I believe we are missing the model of Jesus. Jesus never used anyone for personal gain, and when He ministered, it was always filled with grace to and for the individual. Ministry is about other people, not about us. Ministry isn't even about our next testimony. Environments like this just mean that we will have to make it bigger and better the next year, and our testimonies will have to outshine what happened before. It produces a machine that will need to be fed in order to keep running.

Grace from the church to the world

The truth is that God is always doing amazing things, whether we see them or not. God is always at work, so much so there is no need to exaggerate. If we would just be open to see what and how He is moving, even in the midst of pain we would find the handprints of our God. But we also must acknowledge that if there is still groaning in this world, it means there are still people hurting.

PEOPLE ARE WAITING TO BE HEALED, AND IF THEY CAN'T WAIT WITHIN THE CHURCH, WHERE WILL THEY WAIT?

Where are they free to groan? Groaning is uncomfortable; it is loud, and is usually embarrassing on some level. Yet very often, the loudest groaning is not very acceptable in the church. Through the Gospels, it seems to me that Jesus hung around a lot of people who were groaning – who were caught in, or frustrated by, their current situations. Jesus didn't hang out much where it was popular. As we step into where God has called us, it is the grace of God to us, and through us, which allows us to see the individuals before us.

One of my pet peeves about the church (including in my own life) is where we talk about grace as an option. We say we want people to come and be honest so they can get well, but so often we don't create the safe places for real healing to take place. I believe the church is going to need more and more grace in the coming years, unlike we ever needed before. Why? Because all of Creation is groaning. **With the grace God gives you, He also sends you, and where God sends you is where you will need the most grace!**

I absolutely believe the church will get stronger, but probably not in the way we would pick or feel the most comfortable with, or even in the way we hear about in various church and conference settings. All through church history, the places where the church has had her greatest influence have been where she has served the lost, the broken, and the outcast, especially at the cost to her own lives. It was never, and never will be, about us on our own soapboxes, talking about ourselves and what we've accomplished.

The influence of the church throughout the years has never come by way of her shouting her greatness or taking over industries, or even holding large events. The church often sees those things as meaning that we've arrived, and we often pat ourselves on the back at how we are changing the world. Yet how many people outside of those events are we really impacting?

None of these things are bad things; however, **the influence of the church is not due to what the church says about herself, but rather how the world sees her.** How does the world see the church today? Much of society, when asked about Jesus, isn't turned off so much by the man as much as they're turned off by His followers. Our agendas, our approaches, and our lack of grace are often how the world sees us. In the last few years in the US, where we have had numerous shootings, it has often been the church that has shown herself first on the scene – not to support, love, and heal – but to judge. Shouting about God's judgment being why these horrific scenes were taking place is what the world has experienced from much of the church.

The church often misses the greatest opportunities because we're too busy thinking of our judgment, rather than how we can bring about healing and support. Yet the power the church could reflect by choosing to show up to love, not to judge, is not beyond our reach. But as the fractured world continues to groan, we should not be surprised, but rather ready to show up to love. I just wonder whether we need to change our focus a bit, asking ourselves where the earth is groaning – as where the earth is groaning is where the earth needs the love of God.

When I saw the movie *The Danish Girl*, it was a very clear reminder to me about the world around us. It felt like I was watching just how easily sin entangles, seeing people getting pulled into something where the end result would be death. As usual, as it is with any enticement, those involved are never able to anticipate the heartache that will come when they only feel the pull of the moment. The movie was a sober reminder to me personally that no one is above anything, and that whatever we choose to entertain quickly gains power over us. It is always the little things, the little choices about what we say "yes" or "no" to, that end up controlling us.

I saw the movie with some good friends, and none of us had realized just how deep it would be; by the end, we all felt like we needed to process what we had just watched. During the film, there was a man sitting to the left of me making noises throughout it that sounded like he was identifying with the main character: a man who had a sex-change. His groans were an obvious reaction of pain, but it was also as if he was being acknowledged in his own life. It was a bit bizarre, and heartbreaking, that when we jumped up to leave at the end, he stayed sitting in his seat, obviously frozen with emotion. At the same time, I wondered how many people would see this film and somehow feel a release of justification to act out in areas of groaning where the enemy may be tormenting them. Any time we see where others act out their torment and struggle with the flesh, the enemy has every intention to use those things to attract in order to enslave others.

Our broken places may be different but they are broken nonetheless. The flesh is always crying out to conform to what's the loudest within us. This is why transformation is needed in the first place. The groaning of the man in the film, and the groaning of the man sitting beside me, was a picture of Romans 8. We live in a broken world, with broken people who are in need of deep transformation. These broken places are in each of us too; looking, groaning, and yearning to be acknowledged. Our broken places may be different but they are broken nonetheless. I don't understand how the church can be surprised by the brokenness around us. We live in a broken world, full of broken people; it results in broken choices and broken behavior. I don't view lying, cheating, gun violence, pornography, addictions, and stealing as isolated problems; they are human-nature problems. The root problem is sin. Until we deal with the route problem of sin, we will continue to misdiagnose, or focus on, the symptoms.

As the broken world cries out, and becomes more and more visible, people are looking for anything to fill the hole in their souls. We have to look beyond the behavior, or symptoms, in front of us, and see the person: the person who is groaning, who is in torment, whom the enemy is oppressing. This is a person who is crying out for God's grace; they may not know it, but they are dying for it.

Where we find the loudest groaning is where God loves to shine His grace. Those things we find uncomfortable we often discard as being unreachable or untouchable, yet those are the people, and those are the best places, for God to be ever so present.

One of these places where the church must be grace-focused is towards those struggling with, or caring for those with, mental illness. This is one of the greatest concerns in Britain and America. I hate to call it the "stigma of the day", but it is. Mental illness is not a popular ministry item nor is it addressed in the majority of churches. I understand, because I have led a church, and I know that some things feel like they are just too massive to serve or even too frightening to address. Yet that is our call.

Mental illness is difficult to define, not easy to fix, and doesn't work well in testimony time at church or a Christian event. In the church we tend to categorize people into conditions. But Jesus never ministered to conditions, He ministered to people. When we face areas of our lives where power feels absent, or change feels distant, it doesn't mean that we have any less faith than the person sitting beside us at church on Sunday.

JUST BECAUSE YOU ARE SUFFERING IN YOUR BODY, SOUL, OR SPIRIT DOESN'T MAKE YOU ANY LESS SPIRITUAL. IT JUST MAKES YOU HUMAN.

Christ came so that we can be healed – physically, emotionally, and spiritually – but we are all engaged in a process, no matter what we struggle with. We are all in need of tremendous grace, but we must also remember that our struggle is not our identity. It's very difficult to open yourself up if your struggles have been seen as being who you are, or you have been judged and marked as an outcast, or someone difficult to serve. I have prayed for numerous people who struggle with the idea of being honest in the church because the church hasn't said or been the kindest about what they live with. Most of the time the church is just not equipped, and any area where we aren't equipped we can easily do more damage than good. If mental illness is one of the top problems in our culture, then the church must get equipped to be able to love and serve those who are struggling. This is not something we can just hand over because we're afraid, or we're not sure how to pray. We must learn how.

The church (including myself) often gets stuck in something where God's Spirit has been at work, and we tend to focus on what's worked in the past. But, as the church, we must remember that the Holy Spirit is a person, and as with any person, our relationship will grow and change throughout the years. What God did thirty years ago in the area of physical healing is great, but it is not the most pressing need around us today; mental health is. The power and call of the church is that we don't minister just to what's popular, but to what is around us. Ministry is not what we pick; it is what and who God places around us.

In order for the church to be whole and well, we must create spaces of grace for that to happen. For those who want to get well, but are not sure how to get well, we must become the person, the place, where they have the space for transformation to take place. This will not be done by you and me talking about our strengths and how powerful we are. The world doesn't care about our spiritual gifts – what it seeks is hope.

People identify with our areas of weakness, and respond in hope when they hear how we have found freedom in these areas that they themselves are struggling with. As long as things stay in the dark, they won't get well. Too many things are not well within the church, which means we still have things hidden in the dark. As long as things are allowed to be in the dark, the enemy has a field day. People all around us feel like they are going crazy. People all around us have no hope for change. The enemy is influencing people's minds about suicide and self-destructive behaviors. We cannot get so distracted in how great we are as the church, because in doing so, we are neglecting the world around us. And we will not impact the world unless we turn to God and let Him deal with us first.

Look and see who is in front of you. Who has God sent to you? That is often your next ministry assignment. Where is grace needed today? And as the church we must ask ourselves the questions, "Are we adjusting to where the culture is groaning?" and "Are we ministering effectively, remembering that if people are groaning around us, then God wants to redeem them?"

The brokenness inside us, and the broken world around us, need to know that our groaning has not gone unheard. You may be one of those who are groaning, and feeling like transformation isn't possible for you, because what you struggle with isn't popular. You don't feel you can go to church and share your struggle because it is too embarrassing, or there is too much stigma attached to what you're dealing with. But that is what Paul is saying – this is why the encouragement is so great – your groaning may be deep, but God hears it. You may feel unheard, or even as though no one has ever defended you. But I remind you that God is the best defense attorney and He not only knows your pain, He wants to be your defense. His desire is that even in your pain and struggles you would press into him.

We must acknowledge that God restoring us in fullness will not happen until Jesus returns. We are living between times: between the cross, with what Jesus has already done, and the second coming of Christ. Between now and then we are in a battle – a battle over the mind, a battle of life and death, a battle for souls. As in any battle we see great victories, which should be celebrated, but we must also acknowledge the suffering and loss that come in battle. In war, people get sick, injured, or die; some head into battle and never return. We must acknowledge the victories, but also the difficulties – that is grace walked out. Grace must be shown to everyone no matter where they are in the battle.

Grace is real, but so is the sovereignty of God. The righteous, loving King of Glory is also the righteous judge. A healthy fear of the Lord empowers grace and saves the soul. We must dwell in the place of knowing that we serve this King of Glory and that, in His great mercy, He extends His grace to us, and through us, to carry out our purpose here on earth. The gospel is why we pray, why we minister to the sick, why we need not fear the future. This is His grace lived out in us.

The church becoming the bride she is meant to be is not about her greatness, but rather about the choice of the Groom. Frankly it is arrogant to think that we're so great we can fix everyone, or everything. Only God can fix and heal, but He uses us as His servants to represent Him. The power of the church in the coming years will not be about our outward self-proclamations of how strong we are, but will be about our hope in God in the midst of our weaknesses. The only way people will truly listen is if they hear the message about the God of hope; if the same God is revealed to them, then His power and His hope can also minister to them. The church doesn't need to take over anything. We were called to love and to serve; when our posture is of love and service, safe places get created. Loving people and creating spaces to love people has to be our main call. We have to ask ourselves whether or not we will choose to love even if people never choose Jesus. Real grace in love is not about getting people to think like us, but to make the ongoing choice that even in disagreement, even in lifestyle differences, my love for you remains. Love must be bigger than agreement.

When the church is known for her safety rather than her strength, her self-promotion, or her judgment, then we are on to something. When people begin to run to the church knowing that it's the safest place, no matter what their struggle might be, then we're on to something. I can't wait to see it!

CHAPTER 9

Calling: finding God's will for your life

Then you will be able to test and approve what God's will is – His good, pleasing and perfect will.

(Romans 12:2)

Many persons have a wrong idea of what constitutes true happiness. It is not attained through self-gratification but through fidelity to a worthy purpose.

Helen Keller

Three words that have haunted many Christians for centuries: knowing God's will.

It sounds so simple, yet is not simple for those who find themselves struggling with knowing what God is calling them to in their own lives.

One of the greatest tortures of the enemy is to make us feel as if we are missing out. No one wants to miss out, and whether it is the fear of missing God, the fear of missing out in relationship, the fear of not knowing who we are, or why we are here, it is an all too common tool used by the enemy. No matter what country I am teaching in, or what the theme of the event is, so many people request prayer for the fears they struggle with. Fear is universal and is no respecter of race, space, religion, or gender; fear is often what the enemy uses to hold all of us back.

The Bible is clear about the promise and commitment that God makes to His own about why He has created us. God did not create us without anything in mind; in fact, everything God has designed has purpose. We've been made for significance because this is how God has designed us. To be designed for no reason makes no sense. However, **just because we may not know what we are called to do, or we're not sure of the next steps to take in life, does not mean that we missed God.** The enemy wants you to believe that so you'll stop trying. If the enemy can keep you from God, keep you from saying "yes" to salvation, then he'll spend the majority of his time trying to shut down the purposes of God in you and through you. The enemy thrives on ineffective believers.

Remember, God never leads us to leave us. One of the keys to remember is that even if we aren't sure what God is doing with us today, it doesn't mean that He has forgotten us. Just because we can't see our next step clearly doesn't mean our life is ruined. Never throw in the towel! God is not messing with you, nor is He teasing you. It's weird, but so many people believe that God is teasing them when it comes to calling. They can't figure out what God is saying, so they start believing that He must be hiding, or holding out on them. If God hid Himself from us, He wouldn't be a loving Father; that's just not who He is.

I remember sitting in church many years ago, listening to the pastor talking about God hiding Himself from us. He talked for forty-five minutes about how God hides Himself from us. He gave us a picture of a distant God who likes watching us trying to find Him, but He is nowhere to be found. It's nonsense. That is not what a loving Father does. God is not hiding from you, nor does He mess with you. He came to the world to reveal His love, in order that we might run to Him, not from Him. He is silent sometimes, yes, but He is never in hiding.

If we think about the generosity of God in His mercy to create, save, love, and empower us, it's even more overwhelming to know that His grace has invited us into purpose. Purpose is our calling; something which God Himself has designed us for.

GOD DOESN'T WANT US TO WALK AROUND AIMLESSLY, BECAUSE HE LOVES US TOO MUCH TO LET US WASTE WHAT HE HIMSELF CREATED US FOR.

We exist to be loved by God, and when we know that we are loved and accepted, the fear of being bypassed, forgotten, or overlooked – especially in calling – gets quenched within us.

Living from the place of God's great love to us opens our heart to trust what He has created us for. Everything God created has a calling. Nothing goes to waste. As long as we have breath, we have an assignment from God. If God loves you enough to design you, then He will also be the great provider for what He's designed you for.

There are five areas that can help us to identify our calling: vision and revelation, provision, peace, grace, and God's confirmation or fruit.

1. Vision and revelation

I really believe that when God calls us into purpose it should be so big that we actually need Him in order to pull it off. It might scare us a bit, so that we need to be having daily conversations with God, because He is the One who continues to establish if what we are doing is man-made or God-envisioned. As crazy as it sounds, one of the ways in which I know that what I am giving my life to is the Lord, is that there is opposition to the vision!

OPPOSITION TO ME IS A GOOD SIGN THAT I MUST BE ON TO SOMETHING REALLY GREAT!

If you can do what you see, and what you envision, with your own power and your own resources, then it's probably your own vision. It is important not only to have vision, but also the needed revelation for what you see. You want to spend your life on the things that matter most; for the most part, everyone does! No one wants to get to the end of their life only to realize that what they did was not the most important, or not the best that God had in mind for them. God is not going to commend you on your great plans or how well you trusted yourself. Instead, God is going to bring up all those times you chose to trust where you believed He was leading you. I often remind myself in the greatest seasons of trusting God that whatever I am trusting Him with today, I may never get the opportunity to trust Him with again. To trust Him with our future is a daily surrender that His ways are always much bigger, but also very different, than what we would have dreamed up for ourselves.

It takes God to live in the purposes of God. One of the ways we can tell that what we are doing is in fact God, is if we realize that if God doesn't show up, or if God doesn't provide, then it will not work. When it comes to the plans of God, we actually need God in order to pull those plans off. Don't confuse great ideas with it being God's vision. Ask yourself, "Do I need God in what I'm doing? How much do I need God?"

His heart is to reveal His purposes. "Revelation" means the unveiling of and is an interaction with God. God always gives revelation with grace to His children. He wants us to live and love what we are wired to do, those things which He has created us for. Psalm 25:9 says, "He guides the humble in what is right, and teaches them His way." God's design in relationship with us is to reveal to us His plans. The revelation of what God has for your life is not hidden from you, but rather found in the place of lowering yourself to ask Him for direction. So many things we don't receive because we never do the simple task of asking. God wants to speak to you about your life.

The difference between revelation and vision is that when it comes to vision, most people can sit down and come up with lots of things they would like to do. Sometimes it can be simple: do what you love! And sometimes vision can be all over the place. But God loves to reveal things to His children, as He is the great Shepherd who goes out ahead of His sheep, and calls them over to Himself (John 10). When God leads, it's always from and into the place of love. His love for us desires that we would do great things. Revelation from God is always wrapped in love.

REVELATION WITHOUT LOVE IS DANGEROUS, RECKLESS, AND SELFISH, BUT
REVELATION IN LOVE IS REVOLUTIONARY.

Living life in love is what changes everything – not only for us, but for everyone we come into contact with.

There are lots of ministries which work but were never God's idea. Just because things work, or have power behind them, doesn't mean it's a God-idea. The enemy himself has power and can do lots of stuff. The most important question to keep asking ourselves is this: Is what we are doing God's revelation and plan for us? Are the things that we are giving our lives to those things which will be of eternal value?

VISION MIGHT BE WHAT WE SEE, BUT REVELATION IS GOD REVEALING THE
"HOW TO" OF WHAT WE SEE; IT IS A PICTURE OF INTIMACY IN LOVE.

So it's not just about getting vision, as getting lots of vision without knowing how to work those things out can bring much frustration.

INTIMACY WITH GOD ALWAYS GIVES BIRTH TO REVELATION.

Spending time with God is what gives perspective and clarity to the vision God may be showing us. I am a visionary. I love to think about all the things God can do, because to me it feels limitless. But if I spent my time going after everything I see it would kill me. It would be way too much for one person. So vision is great, but revelation, born from intimacy with God, brings not only the needed clarity but also confirmation of timing for those things God may be calling us to.

2. Provision

God always provides for every area of our lives, especially in our call. In fact, one of the ways we know that we are walking in God's call and purpose is when we have provision.

SOMETIMES GETTING VISION IS THE EASY PART — TRUSTING GOD TO PROVIDE FOR THAT VISION IS A WHOLE DIFFERENT BALL GAME!

By trusting Him for provision, we are making ourselves vulnerable; we're praying, and trusting that what we have seen, and heard, is actually from God. If what you see for your life doesn't bring you to your knees, you're not seeing enough! Time and time again I have seen it in my own life, where God has provided from nothing. At the same time, leading a church, I have seen times where, if it wasn't for the intervention of God, things would not have worked. It's scary sometimes to have to trust God like that, but **God is far more interested in the fact that we are trusting in Him, than in what we trust Him for.**

HOW MANY TIMES DO WE ASK GOD FOR MIRACLES, YET FORGET THAT IN ORDER TO SEE A MIRACLE WE HAVE TO PUT OURSELVES IN THE PLACE WHERE A MIRACLE IS NEEDED?

Of course we love the miracles, but the part where we have to trust God isn't always easy. I have to constantly remind myself that

God is PRO-vision; He always provides for the vision and those things He reveals to us. Why? Because if it's God's idea, then He has purpose in it, and usually the purpose is much bigger than we even realize.

Relying on God, not only for the revelation and vision for our lives, but also for the provision for it to come about, is one of the most challenging things we will face in walking out God's call on our lives. But if we can't trust God with our own lives, then we cannot trust Him for others.

God will take you on your own journey of trust. The calling of God on your life is very personal because it is what God has designed, just for you. Your calling doesn't work for another person; it only works for you. Staying in our own lane, and keeping focused where God has called us, is a key to being efficient where God places us.

When I look back at when my husband Sean and I first got married, and what we had to trust God for, compared to what we have to trust God for now, I am blown away I can sleep at night. But this is the journey. It's personal, because it's a walk of trust with God; He takes us from one place to the next, constantly building areas of trust in us that we didn't have in previous seasons in our life. We can't waste time worrying about something if only God Himself can make a way. All we can do is surrender ourselves to the process of choosing to trust. Every new season, and every new point of the journey, is intended to build our trust in our God.

In fact, **there are often times when God allows our resources to be less than what we need, so that we learn to trust in Him as the source of our provision.** And sometimes God will provide in a new way, differently to how He provided before, because His desire is not that we would trust the way He provides, but rather that we would trust in Him, the great provider.

3. Peace

God's provision isn't just about money; it is for every area of our life. We have been created from love, and to love, and when you love someone, you want to provide for them. You want to make sure that they are cared for. God wants to provide for you, and He wants you to trust and see how reliable He is. God wants you to know the provision He has for you in the calling He's placed upon you. His peace is a guide and confirmation to this.

I have always felt that one of the most powerful ways that God speaks to us is through peace. If He is the Prince of Peace, then wherever He is, peace is. So I've always held on to my own personal rule, which is "no peace, no move"! If I don't have peace, then I don't move. I can't tell you how many times this simple direction has saved my backside! This doesn't mean that it's easy, nor does it mean my circumstances have changed, but peace within the chaos is God's gift to us.

To know God's provision is to live in peace. Knowing what God has made us for brings a tremendous peace into our lives. We are wired to make a difference during our brief time on this earth. Why would God withhold this from us? Why would He not give the provision for us to know that He has a plan? How do we know that God's will for our life is important? Because peace is a by-product when we know that what we are doing is His will. Colossians 3:15 says, "Let the peace of Christ rule in your hearts, since as members of one body you were called to peace."

One of the things I have learned in saying "yes" to God is that even if what I am doing is difficult, if I know that it is the leading of God, then whatever I am doing is worth it.

OBEDIENCE ALWAYS GIVES A SENSE OF GOD'S PEACE, AND HIS PEACE IS ALWAYS A BY-PRODUCT OF OBEDIENCE.

I have never made a decision outside of peace, or in fear, that I didn't regret. The provision of God's peace is because He already knows that time and time again we are going to need to be reminded that He is with us. Peace is an indicator that we are on the right track. Any time I am in disobedience, I lose His peace. Every time I am doing what I believe to be God's will, I have peace; it is a promise of direction as we have it, as much as it is correction if we lose it. The peace of God's Spirit is not only one of the signs that we belong to God, it is also a sign of the favor of God (Luke 2:14).

It is easy to lose peace though because we panic, we get fearful, and then we try to take life into our own hands. Paul's encouragement in Romans 12:2 is to slow down. Sometimes we don't slow down long enough to hear where God is leading us. Paul says it's important that we "test and approve what God's will is for our lives". The word "test" here means to examine, to prove, to realize. It's hard to examine or prove things when you're running!

Have you ever noticed that God is not in a hurry? God wants us to turn to Him, and to communicate with Him in intimacy, because it's the trust in the relationship that He desires more than anything else. God has no need to be in a hurry and sometimes our lives have to slow down if we want to examine what we are giving our lives to, and whether it is God's best for us. Testing isn't a rushed process; it's an invitation to walk through our life and make decisions with God. God wants to lead us, but He also invites us into a relationship of walking things through, together.

When we take the time to examine our choices, it is then that we are able to see how our life is meant to be lived, and God confirms His word by the peace we are walking in. Think about how many things you have said "yes" to because you weren't able to test them properly. Nearly every major life choice that is a rushed decision leads to regret. It's not just about knowing what you are called to, but having the peace that after you have examined the options, what you are doing has proved itself to be true.

Taking the time to examine what God is doing in our lives also gives freedom from having other people tell us what we should do. If we want to succeed in life, we must have godly counsel, but equally, we have to be intentional about whom the godly counsel is coming from. We empower who and what we listen to. You will always have people around you who will have a wonderful plan for your life, but only you can decide which voices you will empower. At the end of the day, God's voice must be the loudest.

IF GOD'S VOICE ISN'T THE LOUDEST IN YOUR LIFE, THEN IT WILL BE DIFFICULT TO DETERMINE WHICH VOICE YOU SHOULD BE FOLLOWING.

Sometimes I have to get alone with the Lord just to drown out all the other voices.

Who, and what, we take the time to listen to, shows what is forming our decisions, and therefore giving direction to our lives. It is vital that we are empowering the right voice. If we listen to fear, then we empower fear. When fear is present, the enemy is present;

his job is to steal our peace. Fear is never the Lord. He is perfect love, which casts out fear; love gets rid of fear. Love and fear cannot inhabit us at the same time. If we side with fear, if we agree with it, that means we are siding with the enemy, giving him space. God doesn't have to lower Himself to use tactics like the enemy uses to get us to obey Him. When God leads us, it is not through fear, but from love and peace, and it always leads us into freedom.

Paul tells us in Romans, "Those who are led by the Spirit of God are the children of God. The Spirit you received does not make you slaves, so that you live in fear again; rather, the Spirit you received brought about your adoption to sonship" (Romans 8:14–16). If we are led by God's Spirit, we will be led into freedom.

THE WILL OF GOD NEVER LEADS US INTO BONDAGE, BUT RATHER INTO PEACE AND PROMISE.

When we are walking in the right Spirit, knowing who we are in Christ, peace and freedom are signs that we're on the right path. These two gifts from God are there to reveal to us, and remind us, that we are within God's purpose.

A LACK OF PEACE IS A SIGN THAT SOMETHING IS WRONG, SOMETHING HAS MOVED OFF TRACK. WHETHER IT IS A MISPLACED CALLING, A MISPLACED DESIRE, OR THAT SIN IS TAKING US OUTSIDE OF INTIMACY, TO LOSE PEACE IS AN INDICATOR OF A DEEPER ISSUE GOING ON WITHIN US.

Yes, He is Immanuel, God is with us, but sometimes we have to be reminded of the importance of holding on to our peace – holding on to Jesus, and getting ourselves back onto the right track. Peace is so important that it is one of the first things Christ said to His disciples after His resurrection: "peace be with you" (John 20:19). The enemy loves to steal our peace because peace is the mark of the believer.

The gospel message is a message of peace. When we head into battle, the message we carry is peace. As much as it depends on us, we are called to live in peace, and more than that, we carry the call to be peacemakers (Matthew 5:9). When Jesus sent the disciples out, He gave them directions on how to minister. When they left a house, if the people had been open to their message and wanted to hear what they had to say, then the disciples were to leave their peace there. No matter where God calls us, peace is to be the mark of the believer. Whether people accept or reject what we say, our peace is to remain with us. Hold on to your peace – it is the mark of God's presence upon us. Therefore, when we don't have peace, we have to stop and figure out where we lost it.

He promises that He will "never leave you nor forsake you" (Deuteronomy 31:8), which I love, as basically God is saying: "No matter what you're facing, I have not abandoned you, and will not ever abandon you." Why does God have to remind us of this truth over and over? Because the fear of abandonment haunts so many. Jesus is also saying we will be abandoned by other things. People will abandon you, even people in the church, but God is faithful, and always present. We need to have such an assurance of this, have it so deep within us, that when it gets challenged, we don't panic.

When God moves us forward, peace is a sign of where we need to trust God. In fact, every time we move forward in God's kingdom we will have to rely on and trust in God in new ways.

This is the kingdom of God in action; if we were able to do it in our own strength or our own power, then we would never rely on God, we would just rely on what we can do ourselves. The provision of God's peace is something that continues to remind us that if we step into obedience, truly having to put our trust in God, having the promise of His peace leading the way.

4. Grace

Faithfulness is impossible without grace. It is the all-sufficiency of God's grace which supplies our needs for where He leads. God doesn't take us where His grace doesn't keep us. God's grace is a mark of His power upon us. Following the provision of God's peace in our calling is His grace. The grace of God is another indicator which reveals that we are in the center of God's will.

Following my personal peace rule – "no peace, no move" – I also have the grace indicator which I always try to keep at the forefront of my mind, no matter what I'm doing. Grace is so powerful and so vast and so deep that I don't think any one person can give it as much attention as it needs, or reveal the depth of beauty it contains. Besides the grace of God that saves us from an eternity outside of Himself, there is also the grace that guides and empowers us as we obey God.

I can't tell you how many people, especially moms, ask me how I manage to juggle being a wife, a mom, a pastor, a teacher, an author, and also travel! The answer is grace. It all comes down to grace. As long as my motivation for what I'm doing is rooted in love, and I have peace in it, it is grace which then confirms if I am doing what I am called to, and if I am in the right time and the right season. How do I know when the season has changed? The grace is absent. I no longer have grace for what I'm doing.

Paul uses the word "grace" constantly. It's how he begins his letters and it is how he explains his reasons for what he's doing. As well as giving him the strength to keep going, grace is what Paul seemed to live his life in and by. Again in Romans 12:3, Paul says, "by the grace given me". It is God who gives us grace, and grace sustains the calling. Grace surrounds our calling; it doesn't just confirm what God has called us to do, but also equips us with what we need for where He has placed us.

Just as mercy, worship, and peace are marks on the people of God, grace is tangible when we step out in what we have been called for.

No matter what we are doing, or where we are called, we only have the grace God gives. It is so important that we don't feel the need to try to operate from a place where grace is not present. It's never the Lord when we fall under the pressure to make ourselves appear greater than we really are, of acting like we know more than we actually do. The false appearance of looking better than we feel can put a heavy burden on us to live up to something that we don't have the goods to pull off.

THERE IS NOTHING MORE STRESSFUL THAN HAVING TO LIVE UP TO SOMETHING OR SOMEONE'S IDEA OF YOU THAT ISN'T THE TRUTH.

Many years ago, when I began to work for the ministries my father-in-law led, I would often hear the murmuring of many who believed I was in a position of leadership because my name was Wimber. To be honest, I think some of that was probably true. But, as John (Wimber) always said, he wanted his kids to be a part of what he was leading. Now that my kids are grown, I understand his thinking; it makes all the sense in the world to me! Of course I want my kids with me. There is nothing more amazing than doing life alongside your kids. It is a gift from God when it works right.

But I have also learned that although family connections may get you somewhere, they will not keep you there! Eventually you have to have the goods. You have to have the gifts and the anointing to pull off what God has entrusted you with. In fact, I don't think it is kind, family or otherwise, to put anyone in a situation where they don't have the anointing to make it work. We set people up to fail when we entrust them with positions where they will be unable to succeed.

At the same time, with the calling in grace comes character. It doesn't matter whom we're related to, or even how gifted we are in an area; if we don't have the character to carry what we've been entrusted with, it is a recipe for disaster.

CALLING IS ONLY HALF OF THE DEAL; THE OTHER HALF IS CHARACTER. CHARACTER MUST ALWAYS PRECEDE GIFTING. ONE OF MY PRAYERS THROUGHOUT THE YEARS HAS BEEN, "PLEASE GOD, LET THE INSIDES OF WHO I AM BE BIGGER THAN MY OUTSIDE REALITY."

In other words, God's grace of what He places in me needs to go ahead of me, but at the same time I focus on building up my character. I pray this because of what I have seen throughout the years. Calling is never an individual sport; our calling involves, and affects, everyone around us, so it's important each of us is doing what God has called us to do, as it only strengthens the church.

While ministering in churches around the world I often see people in leadership who are in the wrong position. Sadly, it's usually because they've put themselves there, or the leadership have put them there because they didn't know where else to put them. It's not fair to anyone, whether it be in business or in the church; to have someone in the wrong position creates and feeds insecurity, not only in the individual, but in the whole team. This then gets fed into the overall health of the business or church. On the other hand, if we allow God to call us, and trust Him to then put us in the right place at the right time, it creates unity and peace within the team, and therefore in the business or church body. It also brings great security.

So many people in the church are in the wrong position because they're following the culture rather than the model of grace that God has set in place for us.

CULTURE FEEDS THE FEAR THAT IF WE DON'T CREATE OUR OWN CALLING AND POSITION THEN WE'LL NEVER HAVE A PLACE.

If we don't make things happen, then nothing will ever happen for us. Culture feeds the fears and insecurities in people whose identity hasn't been settled. Fear in calling is usually fed from the wrong place and the wrong motives. Yes, we do have responsibility to do our part, but **if we force a door open, we then have to keep it open, and eventually it leads to exhaustion. However, grace in calling always leads to freedom.**

When it comes to the church, God's promise to us is that He Himself will build it. Our focus is to obey and build disciples, and it's God's job to build His church. No matter where God places us, obedience in doing our part is vital. Allowing God to call us, and to build our lives, is crucial to walking it out in peace and grace but **whatever you build yourself, without the grace of God, you will have to maintain. However, whatever God builds, He Himself will care for.** Don't you want God to care for what you're responsible for? When it comes to building, God uses His people, but He doesn't ask His people to carry it.

One of the things I of course get asked about frequently is being a woman in head leadership. How does it feel? I always find that question a bit funny as I have always been a woman, and always will be so I don't know any different. I just happen to be a woman whose gift mix involves leadership. How do I know it's what I'm called to? Because it works. As with anyone in head leadership it didn't just happen overnight. I have had to obey where God has led me, and it's been hard work in leading and caring for a church. Leadership, no matter the role, is tough work. But one of the ways God has confirmed my calling is by the grace He has given to me. God's grace is always a confirmation of where He leads us. God uses men and God uses women. In fact, God often uses people we would never pick.

MINISTRY, NO MATTER THE CALLING, IS NOT SOMETHING YOU PICK; IT PICKS YOU.

I don't believe when it comes to the kingdom of God we should approach grace in calling due to gender. I am not called to advance women, but rather I am called to advance the kingdom of God. I lead a church and I need everyone! We need everyone in God's kingdom: men, women, and children. I believe God's grace in calling plays out very clearly when we're focused on the one ministry we are advancing. Within this call comes individual calls of where God may place you, but I do not believe it's healthy for men or women to feel as if they have to prove themselves. If you feel the need to prove yourself, not only will you exhaust yourself, you will also exhaust those around you. The need to prove oneself is operating outside of grace. If you feel the need to prove yourself or as a woman feel you need to be on a mission proving the fact that women should lead, your voice isn't being heard. At least not where you want it to. Male or female, that approach just reveals something in you that needs some healing as it stems from a desire to be recognized.

I DO NOT BELIEVE THAT THE KINGDOM IS ABOUT SHOUTING OUR RIGHTS, BUT RATHER A POSTURE TO SERVE IN HUMILITY.

I OFTEN HAVE TO REMIND MYSELF THAT I GAVE UP MY RIGHTS THE MOMENT I SAID "YES" TO JESUS. I AM NOW OWNED BY ANOTHER, AND IT IS NOW HIS WILL THAT IS TO BE DONE IN AND THROUGH ME, WHICH OFTEN MEANS I HAVE TO DIE TO MY OWN IDEAS OF WHAT I THINK I DESERVE.

I CAN SAY WITH FULL CONFIDENCE THAT IF GOD IS CALLING YOU, NO MATTER YOUR GENDER, IF YOU OBEY HIM, HE WILL MAKE A WAY.

I can also say with full confidence that it will most likely look different than what you've planned. God is not tied to the things we usually are – not to man, institutions, or our committees. If you obey God, then God will use you. But we all must remember the importance of God's grace being a present reminder in where He takes us. No matter where you are today or what you feel called to do, instead of trying to prove yourself, spend your time focusing on obeying God. If our focus doesn't begin "as servant of Christ", then we're already misguided. Being misguided in purpose always ends up backfiring. Leadership in any form begins with the attitude of not only trusting the One who saved our soul, but also where and how He leads.

To encourage the men, I say a few things with great respect. I feel we need you more than you realize. I believe we need some Josephs. Yes, I believe what I do as a woman leading is an example and model to those who desire to lead, but I do not believe the main voice of women leading should come from a woman leading the charge. It is a slippery slope where feminism can take center stage. Being a voice, yes; being a model, of course; but I don't want to do what I do without strong and secure men whom God has called to support, encourage, and lead alongside.

When I go to minister at various places around the world, it is because I am invited. It's always a great privilege to be invited to any table, not because I am a woman, but because I am a servant. The church will need men who are willing to be a bit uncomfortable as Joseph was in having to bear the offence of what Christ entrusted to Mary. This is not about agreeing, but more about covering and loving. I am coming from a place where I did not believe in women being in head leadership, so I have much grace for those who struggle with the idea. It doesn't bother me at all if people disagree.

Whether or not you and your church leadership believe in women in head leadership, you need to be aware of the culture around you. The younger generations have no problem with who's leading, whether male or female. Most countries do not have a problem, theologically or otherwise, when it comes to women leading. So my encouragement is this: if you don't believe theologically in women head leading, get some language and have some tough conversations, because the younger generations do not care much about our church structures, but they do want to serve and to change the world. Relationship trumps organization. You will need to answer, where can they serve? What is their ceiling? And is there a place for them within your church? These conversations will become more needed as well as common in the coming years. The church needs to have sufficient space and place for everyone or they will look elsewhere. Anywhere the church doesn't allow the kids to grow up and find a place in the house, they will go find a place where they can.

No matter the stance, I believe we are better together. The church is strongest when we land on loving and covering above agreement. It took both Joseph and Mary working together to protect, love, and care for the Christ. Ministry is to be together. And to the men, especially in leadership, your role of communicating and protecting is a call we should never underestimate or devalue. We need you! I have met many men around the world who are for women in head leadership, as well as those opposed, and either way I respect their decision. I work with those who land on both sides and I love and admire both. I do not expect men or women always to agree with what I do, but whether male or female, especially godly leaders, I would expect them to love, cover, and protect me.

And I would say to those who desire to implement women more into leadership, don't expect it to happen overnight. Promoting a woman or two does not change what people believe.

One of my biggest encouragements is to get some help. Find some others who are already doing it or are a bit farther down the road. If your goal is to be a healthy church implementing or addressing some of these concerns, then get a support system.

Every week the stage is sending many messages and nothing in the church is more powerful than the pulpit. With respect, those leaders who won't allow the women who lead effective ministries within their churches to lead within a weekend service are speaking the message that they believe and trust women – just not with the pulpit. Yet, again with good intentions, many churches in their endeavor to encourage their women will give the pulpit to a woman outside their church to come and speak, thinking they are encouraging the women in their church. This is a blind spot. Though on some level it will encourage, the bigger message you're sending is, "I believe in women, just not the women in my church." It actually leads to hurt and frustration. If you don't believe me, ask the women in your church who are leading.

The women under your care and leadership need to be communicated to. They need to know where you stand theologically and where you stand in the structure of what you're leading. Believe it or not, this will also bring great relief to you. Anything that needs to be addressed and isn't being addressed not only causes an awkward feeling in the offices and church, it also feeds division. It leaves space for the enemy to work, and we need to be aware he often uses the issues in the church to divide the church. An invitation to the conversation not only feeds the need of being valued enough to take part in the conversation, but also lets the women know whether they can stay and serve under your leadership or they need to look elsewhere. As hard as it is, if they can't stay and serve well then it's not healthy for you to keep them, and it's not healthy for them to stay. I have seen so much conflict within the church on this issue because there is no dialogue. Loving relationships dialogue about the hard things. If we don't have this within our leadership teams, then what message does that send to our churches?

For those of you women who feel called to lead and you aren't under leadership that believes in women in head leadership, then ask God to give you grace to serve well under that leadership or the grace to move on. If you signed up to serve in a local church where theologically they don't believe women should head lead, then not only should it not surprise you to not have the mic, but you also need to know that no matter how gifted you are, it is not your job to "fix them".

I've heard or seen various plans from several denominations, from "secret prayer meetings" where prayers are prayed that the leaders would get where they are wrong, to undermining the leadership in manipulative ways, even using church announcements to make a statement. Media is often used to put men down if they don't release women, often using humor to show men as weak and insecure. Even if that's the case, which it sometimes is, it is never right to use manipulation or division, even using the excuse of prayer, in order to be recognized. When I see or hear such things it saddens and concerns me as to what we're modeling for the younger generations.

I believe that, just as with anything we need to settle within the church, there need to be massive amounts of grace. Grace on all fronts. We are with each other, never against one another, and our love and example should always override agreement.

Where change is needed, conversations about change are never an overnight or an easy fix. Some things which take longer and have several layers need grace all the more.

For those of you women who would say I just don't understand what you live under, let me say that sadly I do understand. I understand what it means not to be heard or to be mistreated. I have served under men who didn't believe in women (and still do and are very vocal about it). I have served under leadership where the men took all the credit for what I built, ignoring me completely in the process. And, I have served in head leadership where I wasn't honored properly, with little to no support system. I have also served under leadership where the men are completely supportive and as I shared earlier I myself serve in head leadership. What I can tell you is that no matter the circumstances of what I have served under, I have grown in and from each situation. I can honestly look back and say, in the areas I chose to trust God and walk it out to the best of my ability, God really has used those seasons for good. At the very least, to grow me up in ways I needed growth.

IF YOU ARE WHERE YOU ARE BECAUSE YOU BELIEVE GOD HAS LED YOU THERE, THEN MAKE IT GREAT. SERVE WELL, AND REALIZE, BESIDES THE LORD OF COURSE, YOU AREN'T THERE TO SERVE YOUR VISION BUT ACTUALLY THE VISION OF THE LEADER YOU'RE UNDER.

I am not saying it is easy, but I am saying there is purpose in it. Whether the leader you serve under sees you or not isn't what's important. What matters is that you are faithful to your God and allowing God to use you and work in you during this season. I hate to break it to you, but getting under another leader won't fix some of your frustrations. In fact, many women believe if they could serve under a woman then everything would be so much better. That is an illusion. In fact, women in leadership can be even scarier than some men! (I can say that since I'm a woman.) If God has you where He has you it probably has more to do with what God wants to transform in you, not in the leader you're serving under. Take advantage of the time as you'll look back and wish you had taken the time to learn more from that season.

I do acknowledge many of you may have been hurt by leadership and my encouragement is to deal with those hurts. If you don't then the next people you serve will pay the price for it and it's not fair to them. I am sorry for your pain and I can also relate to your pain. However, I also acknowledge these times of mistreatment were not always due to my gender, but because I was (am) in leadership. And leaders take the shots.

So we must remember how much grace is needed. We need grace to us, but also grace through us. Grace in the church should always begin with those in leadership.

IT IS GOD'S GRACE WHICH KEEPS US GROUNDED. BUT IT IS ALSO A GOOD REMINDER THAT GETTING A POSITION IS ONE THING, BUT CARRYING IT IN ANOINTING IS ANOTHER.

You do not want a position where God's grace isn't carrying you. Life is hard enough, but forcing life, and trying to live up to what God isn't leading us in, only lead to burnout.

There is a reason why there is a sufficiency only found in the grace of God. He is so good, so loving, so generous that He gives us even more grace to be able to do what He has called us to, the things He has placed deep within us. Grace then becomes a by-product of obedience.

One of the ways we know we are living in the right place and doing what we are called to is that we have the grace to pull it off! God won't give us the grace for tomorrow, because He wants us to trust Him first with today. Being in the center of God's will produces a grace that is just enough for where we are.

5. God confirmation or fruit

When God calls us He also confirms His call. I always ask God to confirm His call in me. He knows how insecure I can get and He is always so faithful to confirm His word over and over again. If you aren't sure whether or not your steps are on the right track, ask the Lord to confirm His call. Believe me – if God is big enough to create you and call you, He is also big enough to confirm these things within you. One of the ways God confirms our obedience is through Scripture.

Another way that God confirms His calling in us is that it works! I think we often complicate what God has made very simple. Obedience to God always produces fruit from God. Spiritual fruit is always a sign of connection to God, and connection to God is what directs us in obedience. You have to look at your life and see: What is following it? What kind of fruit is your life producing? What is following in the "wake" of your life? **Fruit is not biased, fruit is not a gender issue; fruit is a by-product of the choices we are making** (Galatians 5:22). Spiritual fruit doesn't mean a perfect life, but it does reveal a Spirit-filled life. Walking in the Spirit is a picture of action. Fruit has to be produced, which means we have to sow in order to reap. Galatians 6:7 says: "Don't be misled – you cannot mock the justice of God. You will always harvest what you plant" (NLT).

Everything starts as a seed. That's the first law of the harvest. Every achievement started as a seed of a dream. America started as a seed of an ideal of life, liberty, and the pursuit of happiness. Your life started as a seed; when your father's seed connected with your mother's egg, your life began. Literally everything that's living on planet earth came from a seed.

EVERYTHING WE DO HAS CONSEQUENCES. EVERY CHOICE WE MAKE WILL REAP SOMETHING – WE JUST HAVE TO DECIDE WHAT WE WANT TO REAP. YOU WILL ALWAYS REAP MORE THAN YOU SOW, WHICH CAN EITHER WORK IN YOUR FAVOR, OR AGAINST YOU.

Start sowing into your family, because what you sow determines the future generations of your family name. There is the sowing of blessing and there is the sowing of cursing. Your future generations can be blessed because you're planting seeds of godliness. God's reward for what we sow is beyond generous; His promise is that the blessings we sow will still be reaped in a thousand generations' time (Exodus 20:6). Your obedience to God's call on your life not only brings blessing here and now, but for people you won't meet this side of heaven. The calling on our life is never just about the immediate, but reflects the long-term, bigger picture of living our life in light of eternity. Part of this means sowing into obedience with whatever God has called us into, because we want others to benefit from our choices to obey God.

ALL OF US ARE REAPING WHAT THOSE BEFORE US SOWED; YOU ARE
HARVESTING BOTH GOOD AND BAD FROM YOUR PAST, BECAUSE YOU'RE NOT
THE ONLY PERSON SOWING.

You and I need to take our choices very seriously, because our life is going to affect future generations. You can't control the past, but you can establish a godly legacy by sowing seeds of obedience and faith. Jesus said, "I sent you to harvest where you didn't plant; others had already done the work, and now you will get to gather the harvest" (John 4:38 NLT).

Every farmer knows that they will never reap a harvest if they don't take a risk and plant something. It's always a risk, and with risk there will always be moments of failure, but that is not what the farmer is focused on; rather he is looking to the harvest that is to come. It is the harvest which makes the risk worth all the effort. Don't get distracted by the fear of what may not work, but rather focus on the possibilities of what can be produced by your choices to obey God. Obedience is always worth any risk. One of the ways in which we know we're trusting God is that we're also failing once in a while.

WHEN IT COMES TO KINGDOM LIVING, IF WE ARE NOT FAILING, WE ARE NOT
RISKING ENOUGH.

Daily life for the believer involves a lifestyle of risk.

A lifestyle of risk

No one who has ever changed, or made, history took great risks without having times of failures. If the people you follow don't tell you that they fail once in a while, then you're following someone who isn't safe. Not only does every great leader fail, every believer fails. The kingdom of God lifestyle is always about "hit-and-miss".

The calling that God places on your life is about serving the purposes of God, no matter where they may be. There is always an element of risk involved when we choose to serve and love others. It can often be a painful and lonely place to live, especially if at times people aren't very nice! But it's impossible to try to serve God in various ways and do it perfectly, it's just not reality. Sometimes we do this well, and sometimes we miss it. At the end of the day, no one has a perfect record. Failure once in a while (not morally, of course) is an epic sign that we're doing our best to rely on God to do what we believe He has called us into. I don't see any of these times as failure, but rather as getting an education.

I am learning all the ways how not to do things! I can tell you a thousand ways how not to lead a church, or things not to do or say when you're preaching, and I can give you many stories of bloopers in the ways that I have tried to tell others about Jesus. I am a walking blooper at times. But there is nothing more satisfying than knowing that the areas you are risking in, and who you are risking for, will last all through eternity. Every risk in obedience in God's kingdom has a lasting effect for all of eternity.

THE BEST THINGS IN LIFE OFTEN COME DOWN TO A DECISION, WHERE YOU DECIDE THAT YOU WANT SOMETHING MORE THAN YOU'RE AFRAID OF IT.

Many times you need to push past the fear, making the choice to obey God in what He is asking; and you need to want this more than you fear it not working. All through history we find ourselves benefiting from other people's choices to risk in bringing about change for the greater good.

Think of the person who invented Prozac. Think of the person who invented anesthesia. Imagine if you had to have surgery today with no pain relief. Think of all those people who chose to sacrifice the temporary pleasures of this life to take risks so that others could live better. Think of the person who invented the TV or the video camera, or Apple computers. What would we do without our iPhones? Think of how many things, in this last century, have kept many alive because someone chose to give their life for the benefit of others. There are just so many who have risked, in spite of the fear of failure.

One of my favorite stories of perseverance in calling is that of Jonas Salk, who invented the polio vaccine in 1955. Before he found the right vaccine, he failed over 200 times. What motivated him to keep going was the realization that there would be thousands of adults and children who would be paralyzed, and never walk, if he did not find a way to help them. This was at one of his lowest points, yet he decided to keep going, and keep trying. Jonas said this about not giving up: "I have had dreams, and I've had nightmares. I overcame the nightmares because of my dreams."

Risk always follows directions. You want God to confirm the areas you're called to because there is always great risk attached to them. So, yes to mercy, yes to grace, and yes to calling, but how do we know in what area it is that God wants to give us grace in our calling? When people ask me how to know if they are doing what

God has called them to do, I always say, "Don't overthink it." One of the ways we can know we are called and anointed for something is that it just works.

Walking in obedience

Everyone has a calling over their life and no two calls look the same. Yet there are many people not living their call because they've never learned the art of obedience. All the great leaders we find throughout church history were each greatly obedient to God. Sometimes the fine line between those called and anointed by God, and those who accomplished great works for God, comes down to those who chose to obey God. If you want God to use you then obedience to Him can never be an option; obedience can never be a negotiation. The people of God who make a difference for Him are the ones who obey His voice.

Obedience to the revelation and vision that God has given for your life is the key to walking out your calling. These are daily acts of worship to our God. Often we're so consumed with God speaking that it becomes easy to forget obedience usually comes in four parts: hearing God's will, knowing God's will, obeying God's will, and staying in God's will.

The confirmation to God's revelation for the calling in your life, being marked by the provision of His peace and power to walk in obedience, comes with the promise that we do not need to live troubled or in fear. Wherever God may lead you, He is with you. John 14:27 says, "Peace I leave with you; my peace I give you. I do not give to you as the world gives. Do not let your hearts be troubled and do not be afraid."

Just read through the Scriptures and you will find that everyone who trusted God had to learn what faithfulness within that trust meant. This is not always an easy journey. In fact, sometimes it can be a difficult struggle. This is one of the many reasons why the Scriptures are so encouraging, reminding us that there will still be times when we have some of the same struggles as those who went before us. If the saints before us had times of feeling disheartened, we too will have times of feeling disheartened. If they had times of failure, we too will struggle with failure. And just think about how many of the great heroes of faith were surprised by how God spoke, what He spoke, or where He led them. If they were surprised, then we should not be surprised when things turn out differently to how we imagined. These models are often encouraging reminders that these moments of perseverance and struggle, and even feelings of failure, are all part of the journey. The reminder is to not stop or give up on the journey; to continue to "fight the good fight" (1 Timothy 6:12).

No matter where you are in your journey, the enemy only wins if you quit.

Gifts and entrustment

With confirmation of our calling come the gifts and abilities that God gives to us. I think we often complicate many things when it comes to following God. If God has placed a calling on your life, then He backs it up with the needed gifts and abilities to pull that calling off.

Calling is more than a great idea; calling is what your designer created you for. It even goes beyond the fruit. For example, maybe

God has called you into business, and you know you're called to make money. That's great; go make money. But what happens after you make the money? When God places a calling in you, it is a part of who you are. Money is not who a person is. It may be what they can produce, but money is just a by-product of having a gift of knowing how to make money. What we do is not who we are.

OUR CALLING FLOWS FROM OUR IDENTITY BEING FOUNDED IN CHRIST. CALLING IS SOMETHING THAT IS SO PART OF YOU THAT YOU WOULD DO IT FOR FREE.

So whether the calling is business, or music, or ministering in the church or in the doctor's office – whatever it is God has designed and made you for – you know you would be miserable doing anything else! The confirmation God gives to our calling is the provision of having the needed gifts and abilities to do what's placed in front of us.

The gifts and abilities are, simply put, God's gift to us. The church has made gifts all about us: who we are and the great things we can do. But in fact the gifts and abilities don't have much to say about us – rather they speak about the generosity of our gift-giving God.

THE GIFTS YOU HAVE IN YOUR HANDS ARE THE TOOLS GOD HAS GIVEN TO YOU TO CONFIRM HIS CALL WITHIN YOU.

They speak of God's great gift of love to you. But how we use those gifts is our gift back to God. True power comes when we give God our gifts and abilities without any strings attached. In other words, we don't live out our God-given calling because we're waiting for God to give us what we think we deserve; instead, because of God's love and mercy, how can we not, as an act of worship, give our talents and abilities back to God to use for His purposes?

THIS IS WHAT IT LOOKS LIKE TO BE FAITHFUL WITH ENTRUSTMENT. MANY PEOPLE ASK GOD FOR MORE FAVOR BECAUSE EVERYONE WANTS FAVOR, YET FEW ARE WILLING TO SEE THE PRICE-TAG ATTACHED TO THAT FAVOR. WITH THE FAVOR OF GOD ALWAYS COMES MORE RESPONSIBILITY.

If we really want the Lord to entrust us with more, we must be honest about how we are handling what we've already been entrusted with. Have we been faithful with what we have already been given? Are we doing all we can to walk out what God has called us into today? Is our faithfulness a picture of giving glory back to the One who created us and entrusted us with so much? Engaging with God in every area doesn't mean inviting Him only into the activities of our lives, but into every aspect, because this is where our spiritual acts of worship are lived out.

Unless faithfulness is empowered, we will cripple our equity with God and others. If you want equity in your calling, then be consistent. Consistency is what builds equity. No matter where God has placed you today, your ongoing choice to be faithful in consistency is what gives voice to the gospel. Each of your choices to be faithful matters.

Faithfulness is our ability to make the choice to be dependable, no matter the cost. The greatest ability is dependability; it doesn't matter what you know if you can't be counted on. It's a drag when you work with someone who isn't dependable. Think about someone who doesn't follow through. It throws off the whole flow: "Like a broken tooth or a lame foot is reliance on the unfaithful in a time of trouble" (Proverbs 25:19).

When I'm being unreliable, I am only thinking about myself. If I am not serving with others in mind, then I'm being unloving. No matter where God has called you, or what God has called you to, the greatest impact you have in those areas is the love that you show. Being reliable and dependable is revealing our love towards God and others. Gifting without love means nothing. LOVE is the greatest mark on the believer. It is the choice to be dependable in calling which builds equity and the church needs equity. The church doesn't need equity with the church; we need it with the world. No matter where God calls us to, it is the believers who should be the most dependable.

In leading a church, one of the things I have appreciated about people more than anything else is their ability to be dependable. Of course I love to watch people step into what God's called them to, using their gifts and abilities for God, but how they use those abilities is what I have grown to appreciate all the more! The people I can count on, who I know will show up, not because I am their leader, or they like or agree with what's happening with everything in the church, but because they show up as a service to God. I cannot tell you how much I appreciate these people.

On the other hand, one of the hardest lessons I have had to learn is to stop putting my trust in people who have never learned the art of faithfulness. One of my strengths is to believe in people, and one of my weaknesses is to keep on believing they will change, even though their choices say otherwise. I have had to learn the hard way that people who don't follow through shouldn't be entrusted with things in the same way as those who do. Those who come to be served rather than to serve, or who believe their gifting supersedes servanthood, are not the ones Jesus means when He speaks of faithfulness. I have deep respect for people who show up, who serve, and who are faithful in and out of season, and the longer I lead the more I realize why Jesus said trust and stewardship are of such high value in His kingdom.

However, faithfulness goes against the current of popularity in today's culture. It seems these days that convenience and comfort have worked their way into how people want to serve in the church. I wonder if we have devalued calling because we have devalued faithfulness in calling. I wonder if the church has focused more on making Christians than disciples, where getting people to say "yes" has been more important than getting people to die to self? Getting people to say "yes" to Jesus hasn't been difficult, but keeping them committed has been another story.

Yet when Jesus called His disciples, much of His language had to do with the high cost of saying "yes" to the call. Our greatest call, of saying "yes" to Christ, means that no matter where Christ calls us, it is our consistency in our choices – and our consistency is faithfulness of character – that builds equity with the people God has placed around us.

Whatever God has called you to He will give you the gifts and abilities to carry out that call. However, that is only half the game; the other half is to be faithful with the call. The calling upon your life will always get challenged in the area of faithfulness. I can tell if God is transforming me in new ways when my desire to be faithful no matter the cost remains a priority.

IT IS A POWERFUL TESTIMONY WHEN SOMEONE CHOOSES TO BE FAITHFUL, ESPECIALLY IN ADVERSITY; IT GIVES VOICE AND CREDIBILITY TO THE GOSPEL.

Your ongoing choice to be faithful to God, no matter where He leads you, is the testimony of your life. And it's not just about showing up, it's about showing up and choosing to be faithful in the right spirit. I love how Paul finishes verse 8 in Romans 12, where he states that wherever God has called you to, "do it cheerfully". There is an element of responsibility of remembering that our attitude in calling is everything. Your choice to allow God to transform you to become more and more like Him is amazing, but do it with an attitude that whether you are changing diapers or preaching to thousands, whatever God has placed before you, you will do it with a cheerful heart. Paul is making it clear that the spirit behind how we serve is just as important as what we do.

The happiest people should be the people of God. We know how this thing ends. Our hope is not in this world, what we go through, nor is our hope found in what we do. Our hope is found in Christ and Christ alone.

People need to see those who will trust God and give God their "yes" no matter the pain, no matter the opposition, and no matter the struggle. Whether it be in success or failure, faithful are those who are willing to surrender to God and His purposes no matter the season. This is what a faithful person looks like. Faithful people are trustworthy people. No matter where God has called you, be faithful to it. Give yourself wholly to it, as people need to know there are those who are dependable. Faithfulness is so attractive and so needed in our world.

As long as we keep surrendering to God, no matter where He has called us to serve we will find His peace and His grace to be ever so present. This is the journey towards transformation, and as long as we have breath we will be in this journey.

As I look back at my life I can honestly say at this point that if I had known where God was taking me, I would never have said "yes". But when I see what God has done, and is doing, I would never say no.

It doesn't mean that it's easy; it means that it is destiny, and everyone is made for destiny.